BRITAIN
BUTTERF

A field guid
to the butterflies
of Britain and Ireland

David Newland & Robert Still
Andy Swash David Tomlinson

WILDGuides

PRINCETON
press.princeton.edu

Published by Princeton University Press,
41 William Street, Princeton, New Jersey 08540
In the United Kingdom: Princeton University Press, 6 Oxford Street,
Woodstock, Oxfordshire OX20 1TW
nathist.press.princeton.edu

First published 2002 by **WILD**_Guides_ Ltd.
Second Edition 2010 by **WILD**_Guides_ Ltd.
Third Edition 2015

British Library Cataloging-in-Publication Data is available

Library of Congress Control Number 2014954502
ISBN 978-0-691-16643-8

Production and design by **WILD**_Guides_ Ltd., Old Basing, Hampshire UK.
Printed in China

10 9 8 7 6 5 4 3 2 1

Contents

THE SPECIES ACCOUNTS

The species accounts in this book are divided into two sections: breeding and annual migrants, and vagrants and former breeding species. For ease of reference the species are ordered so as to present similar-looking species as close together as possible. This means that the butterflies do not always appear in strict taxonomic order, although they are listed in taxonomic order in the table on *pages 225–229*.

Fritillaries

Nymphalids, Emperors and Allies

Browns

FORMER BREEDING SPECIES (†) AND OCCASIONAL MIGRANTS 160

Silver-studded Blue

Foreword

by Dr Martin Warren
Chief Executive of
Butterfly Conservation

Butterflies are one of the most popular and easily recognisable groups of animals. They have an important place in our culture and are widely used as symbols, both of the beauty and fragility of nature, but also of freedom and harmony.

Sadly, butterflies have undergone a severe decline in recent decades and today almost half our resident species are threatened. Even in my lifetime, two species have become extinct in Britain, although thankfully one of these, the Large Blue, has been successfully reintroduced. I joined Butterfly Conservation to do my bit to help halt and reverse these declines, so creating thriving landscapes that are rich in butterflies and moths.

Fortunately, I am not alone in this task and am joined by thousands of dedicated volunteers and a talented staff. Butterfly Conservation also works with a huge range of partner organisations as well as landowners and farmers. We have received support from business too, including Marks and Spencer who not only sponsor the Big Butterfly Count but who are also working with us and the RSPB to encourage butterflies and other pollinators on their indicator farms. Although we face an enormous uphill battle to save butterflies and moths, I am heartened by the strength and depth of all this support.

Butterflies are extremely sensitive to environmental change and are valuable indicators of the health of the world around us. Measures to help them will allow wildlife to flourish. If you are not already involved, there are many ways you can help. You can get involved in our vital recording and monitoring schemes, become a member and support your local Branch, take up wildlife-friendly gardening, make a donation or even remember Butterfly Conservation in your will.

I have been totally fascinated by butterflies since my childhood, when I watched a caterpillar with awe as it grew and transformed first into a chrysalis and then miraculously into a beautiful adult butterfly. The revised edition of this beautiful book includes the latest information on our knowledge of UK species, both the resident species and those that might colonise soon. I hope the book inspires you to learn more about butterflies and help ensure that we pass that inspiration and joy down to future generations.

Martin Warren.

Clouded Yellow

Preface

Since the second edition of this book was published in 2010, two remarkable events have occurred. One of our existing species has been found to be wrongly named. Another, recorded only once in the UK in 1953, has appeared again.

Réal's Wood White has had its name changed to Cryptic Wood White. This follows DNA analysis which shows that what was believed to be one species is in fact two. The name Réal's Wood White is now given to the French species of wood white, while the Irish species has been re-named Cryptic Wood White.

Small and Large Tortoiseshells are joined in this edition of the book by the Scarce Tortoiseshell. This butterfly appeared in England in small numbers in 2014 as a result of an unusual migratory movement from Eastern Europe. We can only speculate as to whether, or how soon, it may arrive again, or indeed what changes will happen in the future – but the possibility of new species joining the British and Irish lists remains open as climatic conditions change gradually.

Unusual species are increasingly being reported in Britain and Ireland, although all too often this is the result of inappropriate releases of captive-bred 'foreign' butterflies. Such releases are illegal and cannot be condoned; they also risk masking the provenance of species that arrive naturally. For this reason we endorse Butterfly Conservation's *Policy on collecting, breeding and photography*, which can be downloaded from **http://butterfly-conservation.org/files/bc-policy_collecting-breeding-photography-2010.pdf**. However, some unusual sightings are the result of a genuine vagrant arriving as the outcome of unusual or changing weather patterns. To anticipate possible future changes the section on species of doubtful provenance has been extended to enable those species that may just possibly have occurred as genuine vagrants to be illustrated. The most likely new arrival as a breeding species is the Map, a butterfly that is common in much of Europe, and this now has a full species account.

In preparing this third edition, the opportunity has been taken to update many of the species accounts by adding new information and/or clarifying the text. Additional photographs of variants of three established butterflies are also included. The section on foodplants has been expanded so that it not only lists main caterpillar foodplants for each species, but also includes photographs of most of the common caterpillar foodplants and highlights the species that use them.

Constructive comments from readers of previous editions of this book, and the positive feedback received on the third edition of *Britain's Dragonflies* (another of the Princeton **WILD***Guides* Britain's Wildlife series), have resulted in the decision to redesign the species account pages – with the aim of making the information presented even more accessible than it was in earlier editions.

David Newland	Robert Still	Andy Swash
Ickleton, Cambridgeshire	Old Basing, Hampshire	West Hill, Devon

Introduction

On a sunny summer's day in the countryside, butterflies are all around us. Perhaps not as many as in the past, but there are still 59 different species to see in Britain and Ireland, plus a dozen more that visit very occasionally from continental Europe or further afield.

This book aims to help you recognize a butterfly when you see it and to get to know all our British species. It is so much more fun to know what you are looking at when you see a butterfly – and to have some idea as to whether it is common or rare, whether it travels widely or is very local, and what it is doing.

By making butterfly identification as simple as possible, we hope to encourage more people to take an interest in and enjoy them. Enjoyment is the key, since the more people that take an interest in butterflies, the more we will learn and the greater the likelihood that action can be taken to safeguard them for future generations.

The photographs in this book show all our British butterflies in their natural surroundings. Where males and females look different, both are shown, and for those species that breed in Britain and Ireland there are also photographs of their egg, caterpillar and chrysalis.

Digital computer imagery has been used to combine some of the best butterfly photographs available so that the differences between species can readily be seen. The text is written in an easy-to-use style and the information given and distribution maps shown are accurate and up-to-date.

A Ringlet basks in late July sunshine.

Few creatures are more sensitive indicators of the health of the environment than butterflies, and the continuing decline of so many species is a serious warning of the diminishing diversity of our countryside. Conserving butterflies is more than a case of simply protecting individual species, or providing isolated reserves. Instead, we have to consider the whole environment, and how best to care for it and manage it.

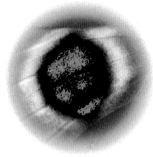

The 'eye' of a Peacock.

Conservation depends upon popular support – the more people that become interested in looking after our plants and animals, the easier it is to argue for the protection of our countryside and its wildlife. **WILD***Guides* is therefore delighted to have produced this book in association with Butterfly Conservation, the charity dedicated to saving butterflies, moths and their habitats in the UK and beyond.

We hope that the book will inspire many more people to appreciate, understand and enjoy this beautiful and fascinating group of insects. And we hope also that you will enjoy the book not only for the information it contains but also for the beauty of the images in it. These images illustrate what you will see if you look carefully in the field. And that is where nature has so much to offer. These beautiful creatures are there for all of us to wonder at and enjoy, if only we will take the time to look.

A male Orange-tip nectars on Dame's Violet in late May.

How butterflies and moths differ

Butterflies and moths are members of a huge number of some 165,000 insects known as the Lepidoptera. The word lepidoptera is constructed from Greek words meaning 'scale' and 'wing' and is now used to describe all insects which have four scale-covered wings. From it is derived the word lepidopterist for someone who specializes in studying these insects.

Butterflies reach their greatest diversity in the tropics. The islands of Trinidad and Tobago, for example, boast more than 600 species of butterflies, yet Britain and Ireland has only about 60 species, despite the land mass being 20 times greater. In Europe, there are some 440 species.

How butterflies and moths differ

Distinguishing butterflies and moths is not always easy, for the two are closely related. The easiest way to recognize a butterfly is to look at its antennae: those of butterflies having clubbed ends, whilst those of moths are fine and often feathery. In addition, a butterfly sleeps with its wings held tightly together vertically above the body. In contrast, a moth usually roosts with its wings held horizontally flat over the body, the forewing largely obscuring the hindwing.

Butterflies rarely fly at night, and many will only fly in bright sunshine. Moths fly mainly at night, but the few day-flying species can be readily recognized as moths by their antennae and resting posture. Of course, as in most classifications in nature, there are exceptions. Dingy Skipper butterflies often rest in a moth-like pose, but they have clubbed antennae. Day-flying burnet moths have antennae that can be described as clubbed, but they always rest with their wings in the typical moth posture.

Dingy Skipper (the British butterfly that looks most like a moth) resting in a moth-like pose.

An Orange-tip, showing its clubbed antennae rests with wings closed in an upright position.

A Black Arches moth with feathered antennae, in typical closed-wing posture.

Some moths such as this Scarlet Tiger rest with semi-open wings, but can be distinguished from butterflies by the fine antennae without clubbed ends.

Six-spot Burnet moths have 'clubbed' antennae and always rest with closed wings.

13

THE LIFE-CYCLE OF A BUTTERFLY

High Brown Fritillary

EMERGENCE

When fully formed, the butterfly breaks out of the chrysalis. The wings are initially soft, then fluid is pumped into them and they expand and harden, becoming rigid and ready to use in about an hour.

CHRYSALIS (pupa)

The fully-grown caterpillar (such as this Brimstone) attaches itself to the underside of a leaf and spins a silken girdle for support, in preparation for pupation.

NEWLY-EMERGED ADULT (imago)

Upon emerging, adult butterflies soon mate.

CATERPILLAR (larva)

Caterpillars (such as these newly-emerged Duke of Burgundy caterpillars) will shed their skin a number of times before being fully-grown.

MATING PAIR

Females (such as this Cryptic Wood White) will spend as much time laying as many eggs as possible.

High Brown Fritillary overwinters in the egg stage.

EGG (ovum)

14

Butterfly Biology

This section of the book provides an introduction to the biology and ecology of butterflies. The diagram opposite illustrates the life-cycle of a butterfly, and the following sections detail the egg, larval, emergence and adult stages.

EGG

Butterfly eggs come in many shapes and sizes depending on the species (*see pages 207–211*).

Eggs are very small, usually less than 1mm across their longest dimension. Although shapes, colours and sizes may differ, the structures are similar, comprising a hard outer case inside which is contained, much like a chicken's egg in miniature, an embryo surrounded by a nutritious fluid. Once fully formed, the caterpillar chews its way out of the egg, the remains of which it often eats.

Eggs are laid singly, in small groups or large clusters, depending on the species involved. The eggs are almost always laid on, or very close to, the plant upon which the caterpillar will feed. The eggs usually hatch just over a week after being laid, except for those that overwinter. Usually, a high proportion of the eggs hatch, although some are lost to adverse weather, become victims of parasites or are eaten by predators. Female butterflies take great care in selecting locations where their eggs are most likely to survive.

Each egg hatches into a caterpillar.

A Green Hairstreak egg-laying.

A Marsh Fritillary will lay her eggs in a cluster of about 300, but batches can range in size from between 40 and 600 (there are approx. 200 in the cluster above!).

Common Blues mating; the female is on the left.

CATERPILLAR

Once the caterpillar has emerged, it uses its strong jaws to feed on plant matter. Caterpillars come in many shapes, sizes and forms (see *pages 212–218*). They are vulnerable and their look and behaviour is designed to maximize their chances of survival.

Many are spiny or hairy to deter predators, some are poisonous, and some (such as the High Brown Fritillary (*page 118*) that resembles a Bracken frond) are camouflaged to help them avoid being detected. In some species, caterpillars live together under the relative safety of a silken web, while other species live within blades of grass that they have rolled to create a tube.

When small, caterpillars can fall victim to spiders and other insects, and, when larger, to birds and small mammals.

Each species has a preferential plant or range of plants that it feeds on (see *pages 194–205*) and many require very specific habitats and weather conditions. As they grow, caterpillars shed their flexible skin between three and six times, depending on the species.

When fully-grown, after a few weeks or several months (again depending on the species), the caterpillar anchors itself firmly and sheds its skin for the last time to reveal the soft casing beneath and enters its third (and inactive) stage, the chrysalis.

The caterpillars of some species, like the Marsh Fritillary (*page 110*), are gregarious and spend this stage feeding and moulting within the confines of a communal protective web, spun from silk. The webs of these species can be quite easy to find and observe.

CHRYSALIS

The young chrysalis is soft, but in time, the skin hardens. A typical chrysalis (see *pages 219–224*) is well camouflaged to avoid predators because it can no longer move and has no active defence mechanism.

During the next few days or weeks, its cells are miraculously rearranged and it changes from a caterpillar into a butterfly, with its newly-formed wings crushed tightly within the chrysalis's casing.

The Black Hairstreak chrysalis resembles a bird dropping and is ignored by predators.

This transitional stage, otherwise known as pupation, is also fraught with danger. A large proportion of chrysalises fall prey to birds and small mammals.

Whilst some species form their chrysalises on fence-posts and walls and are surprisingly conspicuous, the chrysalises of others are well camouflaged. For example, the Black Hairstreak mimics a bird dropping and the White Admiral resembles a rolled-up Honeysuckle leaf.

Others are formed in dense vegetation or leaf-litter and some, like the skippers, spin silken cocoons around blades of grass, within which they pupate.

When mature, the chrysalis casing bursts and the adult butterfly emerges. Its wings expand as fluid is pumped into their veins.

At the latter stages of development all the features of this Green-veined White butterfly can be readily made out as the skin of the chrysalis becomes transparent.

A sight not yet observed in the wild in Britain – a Camberwell Beauty emerges from its chrysalis and waits for its crumpled wings to expand.

ADULT

After emergence, the adult takes up to an hour to expand its wings and be strong enough for flight. Once on the wing, the adult butterfly moves off to feed, find a mate and reproduce, starting the life-cycle all over again.

Many butterflies have a remarkably short adult life. For a number of species, such as blues and hairstreaks, it can be as brief as four or five days. Others, such as the larger fritillaries and the Swallowtail, might live for two or even three weeks, but few survive as long as a Brimstone, which can live for up to ten months (although most of this time is spent in hibernation).

Both hindwings of this Small Tortoiseshell have a piece missing, probably as a result of a bird attempting to catch it whilst it rested with its wings closed.

Butterflies do not grow once they have emerged, and need to feed purely to maintain their strength to fly, find a mate and lay eggs.

Males often emerge before females. This head start gives them time to set up territories, and ensures that every emerging female is mated quickly. Once the female butterflies have laid their eggs, their biological function has been fulfilled. Male butterflies have a priority to mate with as many females as possible, and their patrolling flights are a constant

This tattered individual is barely recognizable as an Adonis Blue, testimony of a relatively long life.

search for virgin females. Males have special scales on the upperside of the forewings that produce scents (pheromones) which attract females. In most species, the wing patterns of males and females are significantly different to allow them to recognize one another.

The main threat to adult butterflies is predation. A wide range of bird species, including many summer visitors, time their breeding to coincide with peak insect emergence. Often you will see butterflies with parts of their wings missing, testimony to a narrow escape from, for example, a Spotted Flycatcher or a Great Tit.

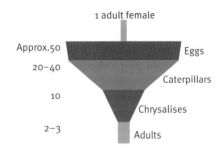

1 adult female

Approx.50

20–40

10

2–3

Eggs

Caterpillars

Chrysalises

Adults

Butterfly survival
A female has the potential to lay several hundred eggs. However, many individuals only live long enough to lay about 50 eggs, of which only 20–40 might hatch into caterpillars. Of these, perhaps 10 will survive to form chrysalises, and of these 7–8 will perish, leaving just 1–3 adults (2–6%) surviving from the 50 eggs.

Caterpillar foodplants (see *pages 194–205*)

Female butterflies invariably lay their eggs on, or close to, their caterpillars' foodplant, which might be a flower, grass, shrub or tree. Most butterflies depend on just one or two favoured foodplants, though some are less fussy. Large Whites, for example, lay their eggs on a wide range of brassicas, including Cabbages, Kale and Brussels-sprouts, but they will also use garden Nasturtiums. Such flexibility has ensured the widespread success of this species, as well as its unpopularity with gardeners! In contrast, British Swallowtails lay their eggs almost exclusively on Milk-parsley, a very localized fenland plant, thus restricting where they can breed. Curiously, continental Swallowtails use a wide range

of plants, chiefly of the Umbelliferae family, which explains why this butterfly is much more widespread in Europe than it is in Britain. Similarly, six species of fritillary exclusively use violets and a further 12 British butterflies are reliant upon only one species of caterpillar foodplant. Some of those butterflies that rely on a single or limited range of foodplants that grow only in specific conditions are put at serious risk of local extinction by any changes in habitat that affect their foodplant. However, others that use mainly one foodplant are unlikely to suffer in this way if their foodplants are common and widespread.

Peacock caterpillars feed almost exclusively on Common Nettle, but sometimes on Small Nettle and very occasionally on Hop.

Adult food sources (see *pages 202–205*)

Most adult butterflies need nectar for survival, although some, including the Black Hairstreak and Purple Emperor, drink mainly the sugary honeydew secretions left on leaves by aphids. The range of nectar plants used by some common butterflies is huge, whilst other butterflies use just a few species. The Small White uses a wide range, but is particularly attracted to both white and pink flowers. In contrast, Glanville Fritillary prefers only a few, usually Thrift and Common Bird's-foot-trefoil.

A Dark Green Fritillary taking nectar.

Camouflage and defence

As well as the perils of adverse weather, butterflies fall victim to predators and parasites throughout their life-cycle.

In response, the caterpillars, chrysalises and adults of some species have developed remarkable camouflage to help them avoid detection. As examples, caterpillars of the Purple Emperor resemble, in colour and markings, the leaves of their foodplant. Brimstone caterpillars lie along the midrib of a leaf, which they closely resemble, and are not easy to find. As well as camouflage, some caterpillars have other defence mechanisms. Some are avoided by predators as they are poisonous, some are distasteful, and others are hairy or spiny and difficult to swallow. The strategy adopted by the very conspicuous Swallowtail caterpillar, if threatened, is to erect a 'horn' on its head, called its osmeterium, which emits an unpleasant smell.

A White Admiral chrysalis resembles a rolled-up Honeysuckle leaf.

In some species, such as the Green-veined White, the chrysalis matches the colour of its surroundings, ranging from green to pale brown. Other species have chrysalises that look like dead leaves, buds, seedpods and even bird droppings. All are a challenge to locate for even the most determined butterfly enthusiast.

The underside of an Orange-tip matches the dappled appearance of a favoured nectar plant.

Adult butterflies tend to be far more conspicuous than all the other life-cycle stages. They have to balance the demands of defending territories, looking for mates and egg-laying with the threat of predation. Almost always, females are less conspicuous than males. For example, female blues are in fact brown rather than blue. Also, the females of some species, for example certain of the skippers and fritillaries, often stay out of sight amongst ground vegetation for long periods. Many species have 'eye' spots on their wings that deceive predators into thinking that a butterfly is bigger than it actually is. The Peacock has the largest such 'eyes' of our butterflies and, if a predator approaches, the butterfly will open and close its wings rapidly to reveal these 'eyes', whilst making a scraping sound by rubbing its forewings and hindwings together.

Living with ants

The life-cycle of a number of butterflies (particularly the blues) is linked inextricably with certain species of ants. For example, Chalkhill Blue caterpillars emit sweet liquids from a gland that attracts the ants day and night. The ants' attendance helps the caterpillar's chances of survival, probably because the ants keep predators and parasites away.

The Large Blue is a species that has been studied extensively in connection with its managed return from extinction in Britain. It is unable to survive without a particular species of red ant (*Myrmica sabuleti*). These carry Large Blue caterpillars into their nests. When the caterpillar is just a few millimetres long it drops from its foodplant to the ground and waits to be discovered by an ant. When discovered, the caterpillar releases a droplet of sweet liquid that the ant drinks before recruiting other worker ants into a feeding frenzy. After a period of up to four hours, the caterpillar then adopts a posture which mimics an ant grub. That encourages the ant to pick up the tiny caterpillar in its jaws and carry it into the ants' nest where it is deposited amongst the ant grubs. Such a practice does not benefit the ants in the long-term, as the caterpillar spends the next few months feeding on ant grubs in the nest.

A red ant obtaining sweet secretions from a gland at the rear of a Chalkhill Blue caterpillar.

Living through the winter

In some species, adult butterflies hibernate, but the majority overwinter as a caterpillar, chrysalis or egg. Surviving the winter, in whatever stage, is a stern test. The entire population of most species exists in one stage only at this time. An exception is the Speckled Wood which overwinters either as a chrysalis or as a caterpillar, the chrysalis dormant and the caterpillar resting at the base of a plant, feeding if the temperature rises above about 6 °C.

Eggs that overwinter have thicker shells than those that do not. In some species, the overwintering egg actually contains a fully-formed caterpillar, hibernating in safety before emerging in the spring.

The caterpillars of some butterflies spin a chamber of silken threads around vegetation, such as blades of grass or the leaves of the foodplant, in which they pass the winter.

For species that overwinter as a chrysalis, these are often situated close to the ground, in leaf-litter or in thick vegetation, where the climatic conditions may be less extreme. Large and Small Whites are two species that overwinter as chrysalises and these can sometimes be found on walls and under window ledges. Butterflies that go through the winter as adults, like Brimstones, Peacocks and Small Tortoiseshells, feed avidly prior to hibernation, so that they build up enough fat reserves to last them through the winter.

Brimstones hibernate from August through to the first warm days of spring in February or March. They hide in thick patches of Holly, Ivy and sometimes Bramble. Peacocks like sheds and dark crevices, while Small Tortoiseshells will often enter inhabited dwellings to find their home for the winter. During the winter, adverse weather such as a prolonged freeze, damp spell or flooding can destroy a large proportion of a hibernating colony.

Small Tortoiseshells hibernating in a garage.

Migration

Though the majority of Britain and Ireland's butterflies are resident, and many rarely move more than a few hundred metres from where they first emerged, a number are highly migratory. It is rare, for example, for Red Admirals to hibernate successfully in Britain, so the butterflies we see each summer are the offspring of migrants that have crossed the English Channel from continental Europe earlier in the season. Similarly, our populations of Clouded Yellows and Painted Ladies are dependent upon migrants from the continent, as neither species is thought to overwinter successfully in Britain. Though the migration is principally northerly, there is also a noticeable southward movement undertaken by such butterflies as Red Admirals and Painted Ladies in the autumn. How many manage to return to mainland Europe is unknown.

Some butterflies only reach Britain or Ireland as rare migrants (see *pages 160–191*). The best-known example is the Monarch (*page 188*), a migrant from North America that is now resident in Madeira, the Canary Islands and along the Mediterranean coast. But several other species, such as the Long-tailed Blue (*page 170*) and Camberwell Beauty (*page 186*), may wander to Britain, often wind-assisted, from just across the English Channel.

There are also some extreme rarities (see *page 160*) that have been recorded, usually as a result of unusual weather conditions combined with a good year for the species.

A Swallowtail (page 74) encountered away from its East Anglian stronghold is more than likely to be of the continental race gorganus, *which is larger, paler and with less intense black markings than the British race* britannicus.

Where to look for butterflies

Some of our butterflies wander from place to place. These are the species that are encountered most readily, such as Brimstone, the whites, Orange-tip, Holly Blue, Red Admiral, Small Tortoiseshell, Peacock, Comma and Meadow Brown. You may find these anywhere. An average-sized garden, with the right plants (see *opposite*) will attract a dozen or more different species during the year. Always keep a look out, as species will occasionally turn up in the most unlikely places. Where there has been extensive arable farming, there will not be many butterflies unless wide hedgerows remain, but elsewhere butterflies have evolved to occupy almost every wild and semi-natural habitat in Britain and Ireland. The key to finding many species is knowing which habitat or habitats they prefer because, unlike those listed above, most of the other species are colonial and are very fussy about where they live.

Living in colonies

Many butterflies are found in the same area year after year as long as suitable conditions remain. Some, such as the Marsh Fritillary and Silver-spotted Skipper, may appear common, often being found in large numbers. But they may be absent from other nearby areas and are rare because they have very few remaining sites. Numbers also fluctuate from year to year, depending on breeding success and winter survival rates. If there is a catastrophic event, such as a major change in land use, a colony may disappear. Even if the site can be restored to its

Different species have different needs

The conditions required to complete the life-cycle vary from species to species. One essential factor is a supply of the caterpillar foodplant growing in a suitable position.

Small Tortoiseshells (*page 132*) need large patches of Common Nettle and a rich supply of nectar plants, a combination that can be found anywhere in Britain or Ireland and hence this is a widely distributed species.

Brimstones (*page 60*) require Alder Buckthorn or Buckthorn (which are widespread in southern Britain), nectar plants and thickets of Ivy or Holly for hibernation. Its distribution closely matches that of its foodplant.

More complex, however, is the **Large Blue** (*page 102*), which needs rough grassland in which Wild Thyme grows and the ant *Myrmica sabuleti* occurs. Also, there must be an entrance to an ants' nest within 2 m of a Wild Thyme plant. Furthermore, the grass must be less than 4 cm tall otherwise the habitat becomes unsuitable for the ant on which it depends.

former condition, it will not necessarily be recolonized naturally if the nearest remaining colony is too far away. If local extinctions become widespread, as happened with the Large Copper and Large Blue, these species could eventually be lost to Britain or Ireland forever. Only painstaking work and extremely careful habitat management has enabled the Large Blue to be reintroduced after it became extinct in Britain in 1979.

Recognising and understanding the fragile and complex nature of butterfly colonies and populations is essential for their future well-being. In the individual species accounts in this book, details are given of each butterfly's preferred habitat. In some cases the information is quite precise, and specific places are mentioned. This is necessary for some of the rarer species because they have limited distributions. For example, you will only find a Chequered Skipper in Western Scotland. Glanville Fritillaries fly only on the Isle of Wight and a very few other places. To see a Mountain Ringlet, you must visit the Lake District or Scotland and go to the right place and at the right time.

The species accounts also provide guidance on timings and locations. The table on *page 33* summarizes some of the most reliable places to see some of the scarcer species. Should you want more detailed information, **WILD***Guides'* companion book *Discover Butterflies in Britain* describes what to look for in greater detail, provides maps and photographs, and makes more suggestions about where to go.

GARDENING FOR BUTTERFLIES

More than 20 different species of butterfly – a third of the breeding species – are found regularly in gardens somewhere in Britain or Ireland. These range from the Red Admiral and Orange-tip that generally just wander through rural gardens, to species like the Holly Blue and Small Tortoiseshell that often breed.

It is possible to attract a variety of butterflies to even the smallest urban garden by providing a few attractive nectar plants. However, careful planting of large gardens with both nectar-providing plants and suitable flowers, grasses and trees upon which butterflies can lay their eggs will attract a considerable variety of species, and help in their conservation. Details of favoured caterpillar foodplants and adult food sources can be found on *pages 194–205*.

When planning a butterfly garden, remember that they need sun, warmth and shelter. Whilst no butterfly garden is complete without Buddleias, many other species will also attract butterflies, including Aubretia, Sweet-William, violets, French Marigolds, Lobelia, Honesty, Lavender, Marjoram and Valerian. In wild areas, Bramble, Blackthorn, Bugle, Wild Privet, Ivy, Common Nettle, dandelions, thistles and willows can all be important.

If you would like further advice, a good place to begin is Butterfly Conservation's website at **www.butterfly-conservation.org** where you will find a section on gardening for butterflies and moths.

As well as nectar plants for the adults, don't forget their caterpillars: an area of coarse grasses (*top*) including Cock's-foot for browns; patches of Common Bird's-foot-trefoil (*centre*) in short grass for Common Blue; and stands of Common Nettle (*bottom*) for Small Tortoiseshell and Peacock.

Butterfly habitats

Butterflies have evolved to occupy almost every wild and semi-natural habitat in Britain and Ireland: they are usually very rare in extensive areas of intensive arable farming, plantations of exotic trees, and inhospitable places like exposed mountains. The key to finding many species of butterflies is knowing which habitat or habitats they prefer.

Gardens and parks

Nr Strumpshaw, Norfolk. Gardens and parks are favoured by many species, with a third of Britain and Ireland's butterflies being recorded regularly in gardens (although not usually the same garden). Though the majority of butterflies use these habitats only for feeding, some will also breed in gardens if suitable foodplants are available.

Hedgerows and farmland

Totternhoe, Bedfordshire. Mixed farmland can be a productive place to find a wide variety of butterflies. Hedgerows and banks provide a favoured habitat for **Orange-tip**, **Ringlet**, **Gatekeeper**, **skippers** and **Small Copper**, while hay meadows may hold **Meadow Brown**, **Common Blue** and perhaps **Clouded Yellow**. The latter is generally the only butterfly to be found in extensive fields of Lucerne or clover. Many butterflies like ground that is lightly grazed by livestock, and so a number of butterfly reserves are managed by grazing. Unfortunately, intensive arable farms have little attraction for butterflies, unless they contain good, wide hedgerows and flowery margins. However, roadside verges and areas of rough grassland or meadows can be good. The best hedgerows are those that are not flailed every year, have a variety of different shrubs and are adjacent to flower-rich meadows. This combination of foodplants and nectar sources is attractive to many species.

Downland

Mill Hill, West Sussex. Some of our rarest and most attractive butterflies, such as the **Chalkhill Blue**, **Adonis Blue** and **Silver-spotted Skipper**, are to be found on the downs of southern England. Usually their foodplants flourish best on chalk, while the south-facing slopes give shelter and warmth, making them attractive to sun-loving species that are on the northern edge of their European range. Many areas of downland were lost in the 20th century when they were ploughed and cereal crops grown. Whilst ploughing invariably destroys habitat, it can also be lost when traditional grazing ceases. Scrub then develops, shading out foodplants that grow in the sward. Downland butterflies are at their most conspicuous on warm, windless days when different species will patrol their territories, perch on exposed branches or bask in the sunshine. If it is windy, most species stay on the ground amongst vegetation. Butterflies, sometimes of more than one species, often gather in the early evening to roost in groups; early next morning they bask in the sun for a few minutes before flying off.

Woodland

Alice Holt Forest, **Surrey.** A wide variety of butterflies flourish in coppiced or managed woodland, although they soon disappear where the canopy is allowed to cover over and exclude sunshine. Several species, such as the **Silver-washed Fritillary**, **White Admiral**, **Wood White** and **Purple Emperor**, are restricted to woodland, but they need sunny rides and open areas to survive. These are good places to see patrolling males and watch for butterflies settling on their foodplants. Several of the **hairstreaks** are also woodland inhabitants. The best woodlands are those that have a mosaic of habitats, including forest clearings, rides and mature trees. Look our for patches of Brambles because these are a popular nectar source for woodland species, particularly **Silver-washed Fritillary** and **White Admiral**. Canopy-dwelling butterflies, for example **Purple Hairstreak**, that feed mainly on aphid honeydew and do not descend regularly, are best observed with binoculars.

Wetland and fenland

Strumpshaw Fen, Norfolk. In Britain, only the magnificent **Swallowtail** breeds on fenland. Our largest British butterfly is confined to the Norfolk Broads where its food plant, Milk-parsley, grows in abundance. Sadly our other marshland species, the **Large Copper**, is now extinct here.

Coastal dunes and cliffs

Penhale Dunes, Cornwall. Butterflies often thrive in coastal dunes and cliffs because these habitats have largely been unchanged by man's activities. **Glanville Fritillary** is restricted almost entirely to the southern cliffs of the Isle of Wight, while several species, such as **Common Blue**, **Dark Green Fritillary**, **Wall** and **Grayling**, all favour coastal dunes. The Grayling is a heath and dune specialist and may be encountered in any dry area where there is exposed ground.

Heathland and moorland

North Yorkshire Moors. Like the downs, heathland depends upon management for its survival. Many heaths of southern England have been destroyed or fragmented during the past century. Even so, heathland provides a vital habitat for a number of species, including the **Grayling**, **Small Heath** and **Silver-studded Blue**. The last can sometimes be found in huge numbers on certain southern heathlands. Exmoor and Dartmoor provide an important refuge for many butterflies, including almost all the fritillaries. The endangered **High Brown Fritillary** occurs on both, while Exmoor has several populations of **Heath Fritillary**. Northern moorlands support fewer species but can be good for **Dark Green** and **Small Pearl-bordered Fritillaries**.

Uplands

Honister Quarry, Cumbria. The hills and mountains of northern Britain typically have too harsh a climate for many species to survive. However, there are a few hardy butterflies that can be found on the uplands, of which the classic examples are **Mountain Ringlet** and **Scotch Argus**. Knowing where to look and searching on calm, sunny days will hugely increase your chances of seeing them.

Favoured habitats

This table shows the favoured habitats of all the butterflies that breed regularly in Britain and Ireland, or occur as annual migrants.

KEY: Common and widespread species: ▓ Principal habitat ░ Secondary habitat
Rare and localized species: ● Principal habitat

SPECIES	Garden/Park	Farmland/Hedge	Downland	Woodland	Fen/Wetland	Dunes/Cliffs	Heathland/Moor	Upland	PAGE NO.
Small Skipper		▓	▓						42
Essex Skipper		▓	▓		░				44
Lulworth Skipper						●			46
Silver-spotted Skipper			●						48
Large Skipper		▓		░					50
Chequered Skipper				●			●		52
Grizzled Skipper		░	▓						54
Dingy Skipper		░	▓						56
Clouded Yellow		▓							58
Brimstone	░	▓		░					60
Large White	▓	░							62
Small White	▓	░							64
Green-veined White	▓	░							66
Orange-tip	░	▓		░					68
Wood White				●		●			70
Cryptic Wood White	●	●			●				72
Swallowtail					●				74
Green Hairstreak		░	▓				░		76
Brown Hairstreak		●		●					78
Black Hairstreak				●					80
White-letter Hairstreak		▓		░					82
Purple Hairstreak		░		▓					84
Holly Blue	▓	░							86
Small Blue		░	▓						88
Brown Argus		░	▓						90
Northern Brown Argus			●					●	92
Silver-studded Blue						●	●		94
Common Blue		░	▓						96
Adonis Blue			●						98
Chalkhill Blue			●						100

SPECIES	Garden/Park	Farmland/Hedge	Downland	Woodland	Fen/Wetland	Dunes/Cliffs	Heathland/Moor	Upland	PAGE NO.
Large Blue			●						102
Small Copper		▓	▓						104
Duke of Burgundy			●	●					106
Heath Fritillary		●	●	●					108
Marsh Fritillary			░		▓				110
Glanville Fritillary			●			●			112
Small Pearl-bordered Frit.				▓			░		114
Pearl-bordered Fritillary		●		●					116
High Brown Fritillary		●	●					●	118
Dark Green Fritillary			▓			░			120
Silver-washed Fritillary				▓					122
White Admiral				▓					124
Purple Emperor				●					126
Red Admiral	▓	░							128
Painted Lady	░	▓							130
Small Tortoiseshell	▓	░							132
Peacock	▓	░		░					134
Comma	░	▓		░					136
Marbled White		░	▓						138
Speckled Wood	░	░		▓					140
Wall		░	░			▓			142
Grayling						▓	░		144
Gatekeeper	░	▓							146
Meadow Brown		▓	░						148
Ringlet		▓		░					150
Mountain Ringlet								●	152
Scotch Argus							░	▓	154
Small Heath		░	▓				░		156
Large Heath					░		▓		158

Visiting chalk downland in full flower in late June is probably the best option to see the largest diversity of species.

Key places for rare and localized butterflies

The table below lists some of the most well-known places to find butterflies that are rare in the UK. They are all open-access sites which you can visit at any time of the year but, for the best time to see the butterflies listed flying, check the relevant species accounts. More details and descriptions of many other good butterfly sites are given in **WILD**_Guides'_ companion book _Discover Butterflies in Britain_.

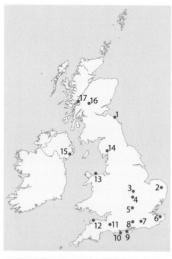

Site	Grid ref.
1. St Abb's Head NNR, Berwickshire	NT 913674
2. Wheatfen, Norfolk	TG 325057
3. Fermyn Woods, Northamptonshire	SP 955850
4. Salcey Forest, Northamptonshire	SP 794517
5. Aston Rowant NNR, Oxfordshire	SU 731966
6. East Blean Wood, Kent	TR 193643
7. Denbies Hillside, Surrey	TQ 141504
8. Noar Hill, Hampshire	SU 738323
9. Compton Bay, Isle of Wight	SZ 378840
10. Durlston Country Park, Dorset	SZ 032773
11. Collard Hill, Somerset	ST 485344
12. Heddon's Mouth, Exmoor	SS 655482
13. Great Orme, Conwy	SH 766833
14. Whitbarrow NNR, Cumbria	SD 454884
15 Murlough NNR, Co. Down	J 394337
16. Ben Lawers NNR, Perthshire	NN 608379
17. Glasdrum Wood NNR, Argyll	NN 001454

SPECIES	SITE																	PAGE NO.
	1	2	3	4	5	6	7	8	9	10	11	12	13	14	15	16	17	
Lulworth Skipper										●								46
Silver-spotted Skipper					●		●											48
Chequered Skipper																●		52
Wood White				●														70
Cryptic Wood White															●			72
Swallowtail		●																74
Brown Hairstreak							●		●									78
Black Hairstreak				●														80
Northern Brown Argus	●																	92
Silver-studded Blue													●					94
Adonis Blue							●		●	●								98
Chalkhill Blue						●	●			●								100
Large Blue											●							102
Duke of Burgundy								●										106
Heath Fritillary						●												108
Glanville Fritillary									●									112
Pearl-bordered Fritillary																●		116
High Brown Fritillary												●	●					118
Purple Emperor			●															126
Mountain Ringlet																●		152

How to identify butterflies

Key features of adult butterflies

Butterflies, like all other insects, have three distinct sections to their body: head, thorax and abdomen.

The **HEAD** is where a butterfly's sense organs are located: two *antennae*, two large compound *eyes* and a *proboscis*. The *antennae* are used for smell and balance; the *eyes* are able to discern colour and are especially good at sensing movement; the *proboscis* is a hollow, coiled tube through which the butterfly feeds. The *proboscis* can be uncoiled enabling a butterfly to reach deep into a flower for nectar.

The **THORAX** is the central and broadest of the three body sections and contains the muscles that operate the *wings* and *legs*. Most butterfly species have six *legs*, in three pairs, but some appear to have only two pairs, the first pair being very small and are not used.

The *wings* are made up of two extremely thin layers (upper and under) that are stretched across rigid veins through which fluid flows. The wings are covered in microscopic scales that either reflect or refract light to give a range of colours and iridescence.

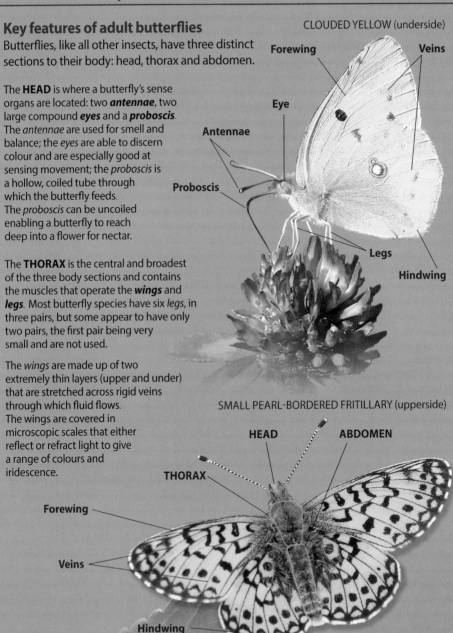

CLOUDED YELLOW (underside)

Forewing · Veins · Eye · Antennae · Proboscis · Legs · Hindwing

SMALL PEARL-BORDERED FRITILLARY (upperside)

HEAD · ABDOMEN · THORAX · Forewing · Veins · Hindwing

The **ABDOMEN** is where the digestive and reproductive organs are located. Butterflies mate by joining the tips of their abdomens. Generally speaking, the abdomen of a female butterfly is wider and broader than that of a male, to enable her to carry eggs which she lays through its tip.

Butterfly identification

Identifying butterflies

The key to identifying butterflies is knowing the combination of features that need to be seen, and their habitat preferences, flight periods and behaviour.

Which family? (see *page 38*)

Working out which family the butterfly belongs to is a good start. For example, if a fritillary is encountered it is readily recognisable by its distinctive black-and-orange upperwings.

Which species?

The next step is to observe its underwing to confirm the species' identification. This is not always as easy as it sounds. But if you have a camera and can try to photograph the butterfly perching, you will have a good chance of being able to see sufficient of the underwing pattern to make your identification.

Habitat and location (see *page 26*)

A knowledge of which habitats are favoured by which butterflies is extremely helpful. A hairstreak seen on elm, for example, is extremely unlikely to be a Black Hairstreak, and will almost certainly be a White-letter Hairstreak.

Flight period

Some similar butterflies fly at different times and this can help identification. A 'golden' skipper seen in early June is more likely to be a Large Skipper than a Small Skipper, and is almost certainly not an Essex Skipper, which does not usually fly until the very end of June.

Behaviour and jizz

Some butterflies have a indefinable 'look' peculiar to that particular species; this is known as jizz. For example, the wing shape of a flying Brimstone is an obvious identifier, even if only seen fleetingly. Dark Green and High Brown Fritillaries have subtle differences in their flight action jizz, which can be learned with experience.

Experience

Appreciating the combination of factors, that help identification comes with experience. For example, having identified a brown butterfly seen in late May as being one of the blues family, a combination of location, flight period, knowledge of colouration and jizz will help confirm identification.

Be wary!

Butterflies can turn up in unexpected places. Species that are increasing in numbers will colonize areas from which they were previously absent. Some rare migrants, at first glance, can resemble common butterflies. Never rely on one factor alone to confirm the identification of a difficult species.

Aberrations (see *pages 36–37*)

Butterflies can exhibit wing patterns that are not typical; nearly all of these atypical patterns have been described in specialist literature (see *page 234*)

Finding eggs, caterpillars and chrysalises

Essential to finding the early life stages of butterflies is an understanding of where different species lay their eggs, an ability to identify the caterpillars' foodplants, and knowledge of where chrysalises may be formed. This is getting more specialized, but with experience you gradually accumulate information about how butterflies behave and their individual peculiarities and tastes.

Colour variation: forms and aberrations

Although the size of individual adult butterflies may vary considerably within a species (as indicated in the species accounts), butterflies of the same species generally look the same. Some individuals occur which appear distinctly different from the normal. Where these crop up regularly they are referred to as **forms (f.)**, whereas unusual or very infrequent variations are termed **aberrations (ab.)**.

Forms are generally the result of genetic variation, though why these occur, and why at some sites more than others, is not yet known. However, although some aberrant variations are genetic, many appear to be linked to environmental factors, such as temperature variation during development. Just a few examples of forms and aberrations are shown here; other forms are included on the main plates. Other publications cover butterfly variants in more detail (see *page 234*).

Butterflies in the blues family often vary in appearance. The Common Blue (*page 96*) has a number of distinct aberrations, the most common being ab. *radiata* which has elongated spots on the underside of the hindwings.

A dark aberration, ab. *semi-ichnusoides*, of the Small Tortoiseshell (*page 132*) occurs occasionally.

Variation is common in the Ringlet (*page 150*), with aberrations ranging from ab. *arete* (*left*) with reduced 'rings' on the underside of the hindwings, to ab. *lanceolata* (*right*) with elongated 'rings'.

Aberrations are seen only occasionally in the White Admiral and Purple Emperor.
One aberration, ab. *obliterae* (above), of the White Admiral (*page 124*) has much reduced white markings, whereas the even rarer ab. *nigrina* has a completely black upperside, except for white fringes.

The Small Copper (*page 104*) has various different colour forms. The most usual is a blue-spotted form f. *caeruleo-punctata*. This is particularly common in the north of Scotland, but occurs occasionally anywhere.

At some sites, 10 or 15% of all female Silver-washed Fritillaries (page 122) look different from the usual females. They are darker, with a distinctly green tinge, particularly on their underside and are known as f. valezina.

The types of butterfly

This section of the book provides an introduction to the types of butterfly that have bred in Britain or Ireland in recent years. The 59 species fall into five groups. Representatives from each of these groups are shown, with a brief description of the key identification features of the group and a page reference to the relevant species account(s).

Large Skipper

Grizzled Skipper

SKIPPERS   *Pages 42–57*
Family: Hesperiidae   **8 species**

Small, moth-like butterflies with broad bodies, big heads and large eyes. They fly with great agility and speed, skipping between flowers. The 'golden' skippers are unique in Britain in that they rest in a characteristic pose with flat hindwings and raised forewings, unlike the 'true' skippers which rest with their wings flat.

Swallowtail

SWALLOWTAILS   *Pages 74–75*
Family: Papilionidae   **1 species**

The single British representative is unmistakable once you have seen it because of its large size, bright black and yellow colouration and the 'tails' on its hindwings.

Brimstone

Wood White

Large White

WHITES and YELLOWS   *Pages 58–73*
Family: Pieridae   **8 species**

Medium-sized to large butterflies that are predominantly white or yellow with a classic 'butterfly' rounded wing shape, except for the sulphur-yellow Brimstone which has a distinctive angular wing shape. The yellows, Brimstone and wood whites always rest with their wings closed; the 'true' whites often bask with their wings open.

HAIRSTREAKS, COPPERS, BLUES and METALMARKS   *Pages 76–107*

Family: Lycaenidae   **16 species**

Small to medium-sized butterflies with a metallic sheen to their wings. All the hairstreaks (except Green) have 'tails' and a distinctive white 'hairstreak' line on their underwings. Coppers have distinctive shining copper-orange and brown upperwings. Blues have spotted underwings and blue upperwings, although females (and males of some species) are brown. The Duke of Burgundy is the sole British representative of the 'metalmark' subfamily; it resembles a fritillary, but is told by its small size and fast, whirring flight. The males only use four legs, the females all six.

NYMPHALIDS, EMPERORS and ALLIES, FRITILLARIES and BROWNS   *Pages 108–159*

Family: Nymphalidae   **26 species**

Mostly large, strong-flying butterflies with only four functioning legs; the two front legs are no longer used and have become vestigial. The underwings of the Nymphalids and Emperors are patterned for camouflage, in contrast with their colourful upperwings. The fritillaries have the pattern of a fritillary flower, with distinctive black-on-orange patterned upperwings and intricate patterns of white, silver, orange and brown on their underwings. The browns form a diverse group of small to medium-sized butterflies which, with the exception of the Marbled White, are generally brown and orange coloured with 'eye' spots on their wings.

Glossary

aberration (ab.)   A butterfly of unusual and distinct appearance as a result of genetic or environmental factors (see *page 36*).

culm grassland   Species-rich grassland occurring on the Culm Measures in south-west England. Culm is an old geological word for poor-quality coal.

family   A unit of taxonomic classification comprising an assemblage of **genera** considered to be closely related due to shared characters.

form (f.)   A genetically distinct variant of a **species** (see *page 36*). This term is also used as an alternative to **race** or **subspecies**.

genus (pl. genera)   A unit of taxonomic classification comprising a number of **species** that are more closely related to one another than to other **species** in other **genera**.

hibernation   The dormant stage in which an animal passes the winter.

imagines   Alternative plural of **Imago**.

imago (pl. imagos)   Adult butterfly.

jizz   The often indefinable characteristic impression given by a **species**.

larva (pl. larvae)   Caterpillar.

lek   A communal 'display' ground where males congregate to attract and court females, and where females come for mating.

migrant   A **species** that undertakes periodic movements to or from a given area, usually along well-defined routes at given times of the year.

nectaring   Feeding on nectar.

NNR   National Nature Reserve.

ovum (pl. ova)   Egg.

pupa (pl. pupae)   Chrysalis.

pupation   Transformation from a caterpillar to a chrysalis.

race   A sub-unit of **taxonomic** classification of butterflies of the same **species** which, as a result of being geographically separated, look or behave differently from those elsewhere but which would be expected to interbreed if brought together.

RSPB   The Royal Society for the Protection of Birds.

sex-brand   A grouping of specialized wing-scales in male butterflies that possess gland cells which contain special chemicals (pheromones) for attracting females. These often form conspicuous patches on the upperside of the forewings.

species   The basic unit of **taxonomic** classification which describes a group of butterflies that is capable of interbreeding and producing viable offspring.

spiracles   External respiratory openings.

subspecies   The same as **race**.

taxonomy   The science of classifying organisms.

vagrant   An individual that wanders outside the normal range of its **species**.

The species accounts

The species accounts are grouped as follows:

Pages 42–159: the 59 species that breed regularly in Britain or Ireland, or are annual migrants.

Pages 160–191: the four former breeders, 11 rare migrants and one species with unknown status.

The order of the species that follows is not intended to be taxonomic, but aims to show similar-looking species as close together as possible.

The table on *pages 225–229* lists all the species recorded, in taxonomic order. The species account text follows a consistent format:

SCALE and SCALE BAR
The scale of photos on the plate is given next to English name (LS = life-size).
Bar shows actual max. and min. length of the forewing.

CONSERVATION STATUS and LEGISLATION
For details see *pages 232–233*.

MEASUREMENTS
Typical adult biometrics.

DISTRIBUTION MAP
▪ = main breeding range.
▪ = secondary breeding range and other records.
● = former location for extinct species.

LIFE-CYCLE CHART
A 'clock' diagram showing the months when the various stages occur.
Full colour indicates peak abundance, tinted colour lower abundance. Timings may be slightly later in the north of a species' range.

THE PLATES
Typically showing both sexes from above and the side, as well as some races, and scaled optimally for each group. The following annotations are used on the plates:

Ad adult

M male   **F** female

Other annotations specific to the plate are explained in the text.

×2 **English name**   *Scientific name*

Former name (in brackets)

Red List (CATEGORY)
Legislative protection
BAP listing

Status in Britain & Ireland

Wingspan: 27–34mm

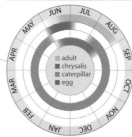

■ adult
■ chrysalis
■ caterpillar
■ egg

WHERE TO LOOK

Suggestions of typical sites, or key areas to look for scarce species.

LOOK-ALIKES

The species or forms most likely to cause confusion.

A summary of the species' status in Britain and Ireland.

Adult Identification:
A concise description of the adult forms, detailing the key identification features.

Observation tips and notes on key identification features to look for are highlighted on the photographic plate.

Behaviour:
Where relevant, aspects of behaviour that can be a clue to identification.

Breeding habitat:
A summary of the habitat preferences.

Population and conservation:
Notes on status and distribution, and a résumé of threats and conservation action.

Egg, caterpillar and chrysalis:
Brief description, with measurements, of the three early stages of the butterfly's life-cycle. Photographs of these stages can be found on *pages 206–224*.

Foodplant:
A list of the foodplants used. Further information can be found on *pages 194–205*.

UKBAP: Not listed
GB Red List: Least concern

Common resident

Wingspan: 27–34 mm

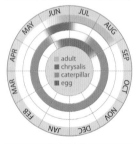

adult
chrysalis
caterpillar
egg

WHERE TO LOOK

Watch for it on unimproved grassland with tall vegetation. Colonies can be found on quite small patches of suitable habitat along roadside verges and field margins as well as in woodland clearings and on open ground.

LOOK-ALIKES

Essex Skipper (*page 44*)
Large Skipper (*page 50*)
Lulworth Skipper (*page 46*)

A common and widespread colonial butterfly of rough grassland and woodland glades.

Adult identification: Despite its name, this is not our smallest skipper. It is best identified by its unmarked golden-orange wings, though the forewing of the male carries a distinctive dark line (sex-brand). The wings lack the faint mottling of the Large Skipper, but check the colour of the tips of the antennae (dull brown or orange underneath) to separate it from the very similar Essex Skipper (*page 44*). This is one of the so-called 'golden' skippers (the group that includes Essex, Lulworth, Large and Silver-spotted Skippers)

Behaviour: A colonial species whose males are highly skilled fliers, travelling at great speed in a blur of golden wings, and frequently demonstrating great manoeuvrability. Females are both sedentary and unobtrusive. It is much more secretive than the Large Skipper (*page 50*).

Breeding habitat: This is an adaptable butterfly, occurring wherever tall clumps of Yorkshire-fog grow. It prefers more open sites than the Large Skipper, often being found in rough grassland on roadside verges, at the edges of fields or in woodland glades.

Population and conservation: A common and widespread species in England and Wales, with its range extending northwards in recent years.

Egg, caterpillar and chrysalis:

EGG (*page 209*): 0·85 mm (w) × 0·5 mm (h); initially white but yellowing with age; laid in small clusters; hatches in August, unlike that of the Essex Skipper, which does not hatch until the following spring.

CATERPILLAR (*page 214*): 20–25 mm; green, with a darker green line along the back and light longitudinal stripes along its sides; the head is large and yellow-green; overwinters wrapped in a blade of grass.

CHRYSALIS (*page 220*): 16–20 mm; green, and formed near the ground.

Foodplants: various grasses, especially Yorkshire-fog.

M

F

This is a secretive species – even at a large colony you may see only a few individuals at any one time.

F

M

Small Skipper's antennae tips are orange; Essex Skipper's are black.

Small Skipper

Essex Skipper

UKBAP: Not listed
GB Red List: Least concern

Common resident

Wingspan: 26–30 mm

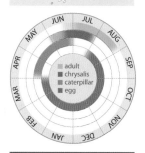

- adult
- chrysalis
- caterpillar
- egg

WHERE TO LOOK

Though first described from Essex (where it remains widespread), it can be found commonly from Dorset to Lincolnshire. It is most easily found in tall grassland on warm and relatively sheltered sites.

LOOK-ALIKES

Small Skipper (*page 42*)
Large Skipper (*page 50*)
Lulworth Skipper (*page 46*)

This 'golden' skipper is widespread in south-east England and is slowly extending its range.

Adult identification: Virtually identical in appearance to the Small Skipper (*page 42*), apart from the distinctive glossy black tips to the underside of its antennae (those of the Small Skipper being dull brown or orange). With practice, it is also possible to separate the two species by the more pointed wings of the Essex Skipper. In addition, the male's sex-brand on the forewing tends to be shorter, straighter and finer than that of the Small Skipper.

Behaviour: A colonial species, and very similar in behaviour to the Small Skipper. Like the latter, the male is much more active than the female, flying rapidly and demonstrating remarkable manoeuvrability in the air. Its flight tends to be ground-hugging, except when courting a female. Like other skippers, the Essex likes to roost communally, and often several butterflies will gather on the same grass stem.

Breeding habitat: Tall, dry grassland growing in open but sunny situations suits this skipper best. It is fond of roadside verges, woodland rides, sea walls and embankments.

Population and conservation: Because of its similarity to the Small Skipper, the Essex Skipper has been much overlooked in the past. However, this butterfly is faring well and has expanded its range northwards and westwards considerably in recent years. That said, it is rare in these parts of its range.

Egg, caterpillar and chrysalis:

EGG (*page 209*): 0·8 mm (w) × 0·3 mm (h); pearly-white when laid within the sheath of a blade of grass; hatches the following spring, unlike Small Skipper, which emerges after two or three weeks and hibernates as a caterpillar.
CATERPILLAR (*page 214*): 20–24 mm; green with white stripes, the striped head separating it from the Small Skipper.
CHRYSALIS (*page 220*): 15–17 mm; pale green; formed at the base of the foodplant.

Foodplants: various grasses but usually Cock's-foot.

Peak numbers occur in late July, a week later than the Small Skipper.

The black undersides of the tip of the antennae are easy to see in the field if you get down low.

Embankments near the sea are a favoured habitat.

Lulworth Skipper

Thymelicus acteon

UKBAP: PRIORITY
GB Red List: NEAR THREATENED
W&C Act: SALE PROHIBITED

Localized resident

♂♀

Wingspan Male: 24–27 mm
Female: 25–28 mm

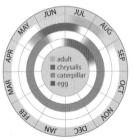

- adult
- chrysalis
- caterpillar
- egg

WHERE TO LOOK

Large colonies occur to the east of Lulworth Cove, between Swanage and Weymouth, notably Durlston Country Park, and on the southern tip of the Isle of Portland.

LOOK-ALIKES

Small Skipper (*page 42*)
Essex Skipper (*page 44*)

As its name suggests, this tiny 'golden' skipper is a speciality of south-east Dorset, although it is widespread in continental Europe.

Adult identification: The smallest and darkest of the 'golden' skippers. Look for the so-called 'sun-ray' on the forewing of the female – a bright circle of golden marks on a dark background. The dark, almost olive-coloured wings distinguish the male, especially older individuals **Mo**. The dark, almost olive-coloured wings, distinguish the male, especially older individuals, from the other 'golden' skippers.

Behaviour: This species flies only in strong sunshine, when it is usually extremely active, feeding with enthusiasm on any plants in flower, especially Wild Marjoram, Bramble and ragworts.

Breeding habitat: Unimproved and unfertilized grasslands on chalk downland, coastal grassland and undercliffs. Areas of tall grass are essential.

Population and conservation: This butterfly has always been restricted in Britain to south Dorset and a few sites in Devon. It lives in self-contained colonies, with little or no interchange between them. Some colonies can be huge, containing hundreds of thousands of individuals. The population seems to be stable overall, although there have been declines in some areas. In northern Europe it has suffered a serious decline, but remains relatively abundant on calcareous grassland further south and east.

Egg, caterpillar and chrysalis:
EGG (*page 209*): 1·6 mm (w) × 0·8 mm (h); pale and oblong; laid in rows on the flower sheath of its foodplant.
CATERPILLAR (*page 214*): 25 mm; green, with a darker green line along the middle of the back and pale yellowish lines on either side; it is usually hidden in a blade of grass curled round to form a feeding tube; overwinters without feeding.
CHRYSALIS (*page 220*): 17 mm; pale green and hidden in a tussock of grass.

Foodplant: Tor-grass.

Look for the distinctive circle of golden markings on the female's forewing.

Look for this species on hot summer days – it is at its most abundant in early to mid-August.

Lulworth Skipper habitat – a south-facing slope sheltered from onshore winds in coastal Dorset.

Silver-spotted Skipper   *Hesperia comma*

UKBAP: Not listed
GB Red List: Near Threatened
W&C Act: Sale Prohibited

Localized resident

Wingspan   Male: 29–34 mm
Female: 32–37 mm

♂♀

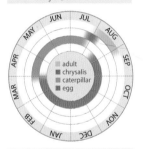

- adult
- chrysalis
- caterpillar
- egg

WHERE TO LOOK

Sheltered chalk downland with tightly-grazed turf and patches of bare ground for basking. Reliable sites include Aston Rowant in Oxfordshire, Malling Down in East Sussex and Martin Down in Hampshire.

LOOK-ALIKES

Large Skipper (*page 50*)

A rare and localized 'golden' skipper, characteristic of the chalk downlands of southern England, which marks the northern edge of its European range.

Adult identification: Both sexes are readily identified by the silver spots on the underside of each hindwing, easily seen when the butterfly is at rest. These markings are the best way to separate it from the Large Skipper (*page 50*), with which it is most likely to be confused. However, the flight periods of the two species hardly overlap: the Silver-spotted being the last of the skippers to emerge, usually not appearing until the second week of August, by which time most Large Skippers have disappeared.

Behaviour: This is a sun-loving species that spends much of its short adult life basking on bare ground. It holds its wings in the characteristic 'V' of all 'golden' skippers. The flight is fast and darting, close to the ground, stopping to feed on late-summer flowers such as Dwarf Thistle and knapweeds.

Breeding habitat: Open chalk grassland with a short, sparse turf – conditions generally created through heavy grazing by sheep or rabbits. It is usually found on south-facing slopes, but if the conditions are warm enough it will also occur on other scarps.

Population and conservation: This butterfly has always been restricted to chalk and limestone grassland. It declined drastically from about 1950, but has since recovered. Grazing is essential and scrub control is important for the maintenance of optimal habitat. The current upward population trend is thought to be due to effective conservation management and, possibly, to warmer weather conditions.

Egg, caterpillar and chrysalis:
Egg (*page 209*): 0·9 mm (w) × 0·7 mm (h); off-white.
Caterpillar (*page 214*): 25 mm; brownish-green and grub-like, spinning its own silk nest.
Chrysalis (*page 220*): 15 mm; dark olive-green, protected by a cocoon in a grass tussock.

Foodplant: Sheep's-fescue.

Look for the distinctive silver spots on the underside of the hindwings.

Best looked for when basking on bare ground on hot, sunny days in late August.

Grazed, open, south-facing chalk grassland is the preferred habitat.

Large Skipper *Ochlodes sylvanus*

UKBAP: Not listed
GB Red List: Least concern

Common resident

Wingspan Male: 29–34 mm
Female: 31–36 mm

♂♀

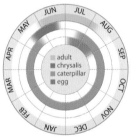

- adult
- chrysalis
- caterpillar
- egg

WHERE TO LOOK

An easy species to find in the right habitat anywhere in England, north to just over the Scottish border, and throughout Wales, but not in Ireland.

LOOK-ALIKES

Small Skipper (*page 42*)
Essex Skipper (*page 44*)
Silver-spotted Skipper (*page 48*)

This 'golden' skipper is widespread throughout much of England and Wales, extending northwards to southern Scotland, and is common on rough grassland in lowland regions. It has not been recorded in Ireland.

Adult identification: Though it is somewhat larger than both the Small (*page 42*) and Essex Skippers (*page 44*), size is not the easiest identification feature. Look instead for the faint chequered pattern on both sides of the wings. The male can be told readily from the female by the prominent dark line (sex-brand) on the forewing.

Behaviour: Males spend sunny mornings patrolling in search of receptive females, and afternoons basking in the sun in the characteristic skipper 'V' pose. Favoured perches are usually close to the ground, from which males launch brief, fierce attacks on rival males, or intercept passing females. Females are unobtrusive and, once mated, spend most of their time resting, being active only when egg-laying or feeding. On cool days, males may patrol later in the day, probably because the emergence of fresh females is delayed.

Breeding habitat: As long as its requirement for tall, uncut long grasses can be met, this species is happy in a wide variety of habitats. These range from woodland rides and rough grassland to roadside verges and hedgerows, though it also inhabits urban parks and churchyards.

Population and conservation: This species gradually spread into northern counties and the borders in the second half of the 20th century. Although its range now appears to be stable, the requirement for uncut grasses means that intensive agriculture has led to the loss of many established colonies and the overall population has decreased.

Egg, caterpillar and chrysalis:

EGG (*page 209*): 1·1 mm (w) × 0·8 mm (h); dome-shaped; dull white; laid singly, usually on underside of a grass blade.
CATERPILLAR (*page 214*): 28 mm; bluish-green, with a dark line along the back and a yellowish line along the flank; lives inside a grass blade bound into a tube by silken threads and only ventures out to feed.
CHRYSALIS (*page 220*): 19 mm; dark, dusted with a white, waxy powder.

Foodplants: various grasses but normally Cock's-foot.

Both sexes have a faint chequered pattern on both the undersides and uppersides of the wings.

Most active on hot days, and most numerous in mid-July.

Any location with tall grasses may hold colonies.

Chequered Skipper   *Carterocephalus palaemon*

UKBAP: PRIORITY
GB Red List: ENDANGERED
W&C Act: SALE PROHIBITED

Declining resident

♂♀ | **Wingspan** | Male: | 29 mm
| | Female: | 31 mm

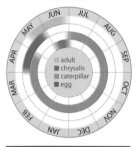

WHERE TO LOOK

Western Scotland around Fort William, where there are some 40 known colonies including Glasdrum Wood on the north shore of Loch Creran, and Allt Mhuic, west of Spean Bridge.

LOOK-ALIKES

Duke of Burgundy (*page 106*)

Though sadly extinct in England since 1976, small colonies of this attractive skipper can still be found in western Scotland.

Adult identification: With its distinctive chequered cream-on-chocolate wings, this is one of the easiest of our skippers to identify. The only possible confusion is with the Duke of Burgundy (*page 106*), but the latter has a distinctively different shape and is spotted rather than chequered, and its British range is nowhere near that of the Chequered Skipper.

Behaviour: The male establishes a small territory, darting from his favoured perch in a blur of wings to investigate intruders. Like all skippers, the flight is fast and dashing, with sudden changes of direction. Both sexes visit flowers, and seem particularly keen on blue or mauve species, including Bugle, Bluebell and Marsh Thistle. Females sometimes stray when looking for egg-laying sites.

BREEDING HABITAT

Scottish colonies are generally in open grassland on the edge of broad-leaved woodland. Wet but not waterlogged soils are preferred, and most breeding areas are found close to the base of a slope, usually close to a loch or river. In England, this species used to favour woodland rides and clearings.

Population and conservation: Once a scarce but quite widespread species in the English Midlands, the last known colony died out in about 1976 and subsequent reintroductions have, so far, been unsuccessful. The Scottish colonies, first discovered in 1942, seem to be holding their own in ten core areas.

Egg, caterpillar and chrysalis:
EGG (*page 209*): 0·6 mm (w) × 0·5 mm (h); off-white; laid singly on the underside of selected blades of grass.

CATERPILLAR (*page 214*): 25 mm; changes colour during the year, starting with a base colour of pale green before winter hibernation; after hibernation, it turns straw-coloured.

CHRYSALIS (*page 220*): 16 mm; hidden amongst dried grass and yellow/grey in colour, it resembles a dead blade of grass and is very difficult to find.

Foodplant: Purple Moor-grass.

Best looked for in late May, when numbers peak; fine weather is best for success.

In wet weather it is still worth checking flower-heads for resting adults.

Typical Scottish Chequered Skipper habitat.

Grizzled Skipper

Pyrgus malvae

Declining resident

Wingspan: 23–29 mm

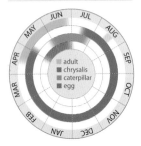

adult
chrysalis
caterpillar
egg

WHERE TO LOOK

Most large colonies are on nature reserves.
Reliable sites are Martin Down in Hampshire, Park Corner Heath in East Sussex, Cerne Giant Hill in Dorset, Twywell Hills and Dales in Northamptonshire, and Merthyr Mawr in Glamorganshire.

LOOK-ALIKES

Dingy Skipper (*page 56*)

This skipper is a spring butterfly, found most commonly on our southern chalk downlands. It is a declining species throughout much of its range.

Adult identification: Tiny and rather moth-like, this skipper is readily identified by its pattern of white chequers on dark wings, with distinctive black-and-white fringes. The male and female are very similar in appearance. The ground colour of newly-emerged butterflies can be almost black.

Behaviour: This species has the typical, rapid flight of the skippers, usually keeping close to the ground, but it is one of the most accomplished fliers; battles between rival males include spectacular displays of flying skills. Males like to bask in the sun in favoured sheltered hollows, every now and again darting off at speed to attack a rival or court a female. There is occasionally a second generation in August.

Breeding habitat: Though usually thought of as a butterfly of chalk downland, this species can also be found in a wide variety of other sites, from woodland rides and waste ground to railway lines. The chief requirement appears to be a plentiful supply of foodplants, patches of bare ground, and an abundance of spring nectar plants.

Population and conservation: A declining species that has suffered from habitat loss due to changing patterns of land use. It typically lives in small, self-contained colonies and populations have been shown to respond positively to conservation management involving coppicing and the introduction of suitable grazing.

Egg, caterpillar and chrysalis:
EGG (*page 209*): 0·6 mm (w) × 0·5 mm (h); bun-shaped; pale; laid singly on the foodplant.
CATERPILLAR (*page 214*): 18 mm; ochreous-green with thin olive stripes and a prominent black head.
CHRYSALIS (*page 220*): 13 mm; predominantly brown, with light and dark markings. It is formed near the ground and protected by a silken cocoon.

Foodplants: Wild Strawberry, Agrimony, Creeping Cinquefoil, and sometimes Tormentil, Bramble, Salad Burnet.

A rare form, taras, in which the white forewing markings spread out and merge to form larger white spots, is found at a few sites.

Best looked for on hot days in late May and early June, especially where Wild Strawberry grows. Watch carefully for the sudden darting movements of males of this small butterfly.

Small colonies are most likely in habitats with patches of bare ground and plentiful foodplants.

Dingy Skipper

Erynnis tages

UKBAP: Priority
GB Red List: Vulnerable
Wildlife (NI) Order: Protected
Localized resident

| Wingspan: | 27–34mm |

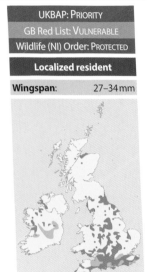

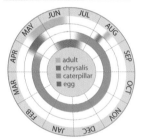

- adult
- chrysalis
- caterpillar
- egg

WHERE TO LOOK

Occurs at many sites, with strongholds in the southern downlands. Martin Down and Magdalen Hill Down in Hampshire are reliable sites. In Ireland, The Burren in County Clare is a favoured locality.

LOOK-ALIKES

Grizzled Skipper (*page 54*)
Mother Shipton moth
(*opposite*)
Burnet Companion moth
(*opposite*)

This beautifully camouflaged species has a highly localized distribution in the British Isles, and has declined seriously in recent years. It is the only skipper found in Ireland.

Adult identification: The sexes are very similar, with brown wings that can cause confusion with the day-flying Mother Shipton (*opposite, top inset*) and Burnet Companion (*opposite, bottom inset*) moths, and also the Grizzled Skipper (*page 54*). The latter differs in having an obvious pattern of black and white squares on its wings. As adults age, they lose wing scales and become duller and paler. Butterflies found in The Burren and south-east Galway in western Ireland (race *baynesi*) have an upperside with more subdued pale markings on a grey-brown background.

Behaviour: This butterfly spends much of the day basking, with wings wide open, on patches of bare ground, where they can be easily overlooked. It is a fast flier, the males chasing passing females and sometimes towering high into the sky. A roosting Dingy Skipper looks most moth-like because of its curious way of perching with its wings curved in a manner unlike any other British butterfly.

Breeding habitat: Favours a variety of open sunny habitats, being found on chalk downland, heathland, railway lines, disused quarries and waste ground. It favours areas with a combination of bare earth and taller vegetation for roosting.

Population and conservation: The worrying decline in the population of this species in recent years seems to be almost entirely due to loss of habitat. Conservation management involving extensive grazing and scrub clearance has been shown to help reverse this decline. Many sites in the Midlands rely on the protection of post-industrial 'brownfield' sites.

Egg, caterpillar and chrysalis:
Egg (*page 209*): 0·5mm(w) × 0·5mm(h); green, soon turning orange; laid singly.
Caterpillar (*page 214*): 17mm; green, with a dark green line along back and a distinctive dark head.
Chrysalis (*page 220*): 14mm; brown; formed in the spring, with the adult emerging a month later.

Foodplant: usually Common Bird's-foot-trefoil.

M

M

F

M

Somewhat moth-like (see below) in some poses.

F

Found on warm, south-facing slopes, most readily in late May.

Mother Shipton moth (×1½)

Open, sunny habitats, such as disused
railway lines are good places to search.

Burnet Companion moth (×1½)

Clouded Yellow

Colias croceus

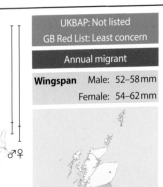

| UKBAP: Not listed |
| GB Red List: Least concern |
| **Annual migrant** |

| **Wingspan** | Male: 52–58 mm |
| | Female: 54–62 mm |

♂♀

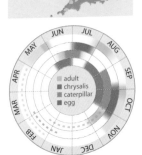

- adult
- chrysalis
- caterpillar
- egg

WHERE TO LOOK

Often common on the South Downs, and can also be seen occasionally anywhere, especially on fields of clover. In a poor year, they often do not stray far from the south coast.

LOOK-ALIKES

Brimstone (*page 60*)
Whites (*pages 62–72*)
Other clouded yellows
  (*pages 166–167*)

This beautiful golden-yellow butterfly is an annual migrant to Britain and Ireland. Numbers vary enormously from year to year, with exceptional 'Clouded Yellow summers' typically occurring once in a decade.

Adult identification: With its rich, chrome-yellow wings heavily edged in black, the Clouded Yellow is one of the easiest butterflies to identify. The female is normally slightly darker than the male, and her wing margins are dotted with yellow spots. Some 10% of females are of the pale form, *helice*, their colour ranging from a soft lemon-yellow to white. The distinctive underwing pattern is similar in both the normal and *helice* forms.

Behaviour: A highly migratory species that reaches our shores every year. Good years occur often but Clouded Yellows are only really abundant about once every decade, such as in 2013, when fields of clover fill with these beautiful butterflies. They are powerful fliers, travelling fast and low, and when they pause to feed, they invariably do so with their wings closed. The breeding cycle is extremely rapid: an egg laid in early June may produce an adult butterfly by mid-July.

Breeding habitat: As wandering migrants, Clouded Yellows can occur anywhere, but they favour chalk downlands, and are one of the few butterflies that like extensive fields of clover and Lucerne.

Population and conservation: The size of the British population depends entirely on how many migrate here. Recently, there have been indications that the species has overwintered on the Isle of Wight and near Beachy Head, but generally the British winter is too cold and wet for it to survive. In a good summer, the population can be measured in millions, while in other years it may just be hundreds.

Egg, caterpillar and chrysalis:
EGG (*page 207*): 0·4 mm (w) × 1·1 mm (h); bottle-shaped; whitish-yellow, turning pinkish; laid singly.
CATERPILLAR (*page 212*): 33 mm; green, speckled with black, and with a fine yellow line along each side.
CHRYSALIS (*page 219*): 22 mm; green, with a pale yellow stripe on the back and black spots on the underside at the rear end.

Foodplants: clovers, Lucerne or Common Bird's-foot-trefoil.

The uppersides are normally only seen in flight; the yellow spots on the black wing margins distinguish the female.

Early migrants may arrive by May or June, but August and early September are the best times to look.

The form helice is similar to the very rare Berger's and Pale Clouded Yellows (pages 166–167).

f. helice

A backlit female's 'spots' are easy to see.

UKBAP: Not listed
GB Red List: Least concern
Wildlife (NI) Order: PROTECTED

Widespread resident

Wingspan: 60–74 mm

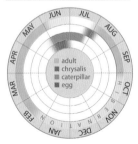

- adult
- chrysalis
- caterpillar
- egg

WHERE TO LOOK

Can be found almost anywhere from early spring to late summer, but does not occur as far north as the Large White.

LOOK-ALIKES

Large White (*page 62*)
Clouded Yellow (*page 58*)

This is the original 'butter-coloured fly'. Although mainly found in southern and central England, it is also common in Ireland and is slowly extending its range northwards.

Adult identification: Males, with their sulphur-yellow wings, are difficult to confuse with any other British butterfly. Their wandering flight is usually high and conspicuous, totally unlike the fast, low flight of a Clouded Yellow (*page 58*), the only other yellow butterfly seen regularly in Britain and Ireland. The female is a very pale lemon or greenish yellow, and can, at a distance, be confused with a Large White (*page 62*). However the Brimstone has no black on its wings. When perched, the leaf-like wing shape is diagnostic. Butterflies in Ireland (race *gravesi*) are slightly paler and have a more greenish tinge.

Behaviour: Warm, sunny days in early March rouse Brimstones from their hibernation, patrolling males usually being one of the first signs of spring. Though there is only one generation a year, this is such a long-lived species that adults may be seen on the wing in almost every month. Mating takes place only in the spring, when the spiralling courtship flight is a familiar sight. Brimstones always shut their wings when resting or feeding.

Breeding habitat: This lovely butterfly favours scrubby woodland and hedgerows where its foodplants grow.

Population and conservation: The range of this species in Britain and Ireland is limited by the availability of its caterpillars' foodplants. It is increasingly being recorded at the northern edge of its range, possibly because more Buckthorn is being used in hedgerow planting and in gardens. However, the total population has probably declined in line with the destruction of hedgerows during the second half of the 20th century.

Egg, caterpillar and chrysalis:
EGG (*page 207*): 0·5 mm (w) × 1·3 mm (h); lozenge-shaped; very pale green when first laid, becoming darker; usually placed on the underside of leaves but sometimes on or near new buds before the leaves open.
CATERPILLAR (*page 212*): 32–34 mm; green, finely speckled with black, and with a white line of spiracles.
CHRYSALIS (*page 219*): 22–24 mm; leaf-like in shape and colour.

Foodplants: Buckthorn and Alder Buckthorn.

M

The sulphur-yellow males are no problem to identify, but be wary of the similarities between female Brimstones and Large Whites.

F

Large White

Pieris brassicae

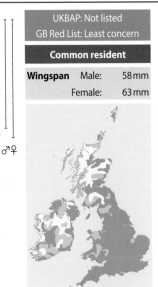

UKBAP: Not listed	
GB Red List: Least concern	

Common resident

Wingspan	Male:	58 mm
	Female:	63 mm

♂♀

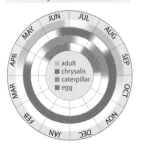

adult
chrysalis
caterpillar
egg

WHERE TO LOOK

Open ground, farmland and gardens, almost anywhere except on high mountain tops. Also look out for migrants heading north in the spring.

LOOK-ALIKES

Brimstone (*page 60*)
Small White (*page 64*)
Green-veined White (*page 66*)

Our largest white butterfly. This and the similar looking Small White are the two species most disliked by gardeners who usually refer to them as 'Cabbage Whites' without distinction. Numbers vary from year to year, depending partly on migration from continental Europe.

Adult identification: The female in particular is a handsome insect, with a conspicuous pair of black dots on her forewings, and a faint pale-yellow wash to the upperside of the hindwing. Males lack the black dots and yellow tinge to the upperside, but both sexes have similar undersides. Males are smaller than females; a small male is practically the same size as many Small Whites (*page 64*). However, Large Whites always have more extensive black tips to their wings. There are two or sometimes three generations a year, with summer butterflies often having stronger black markings on their upperwings and paler underwings than those of the spring generation.

Behaviour: Our resident population is reinforced annually with migrants from continental Europe. When migrating, they may fly at up to 15 km/h given favourable wind conditions, but once settled in an area their flight is typically much more relaxed.

Breeding habitat: A widespread and adaptable butterfly that occurs as far north as Shetland. Though it can be encountered almost anywhere, it particularly likes gardens and allotments where Cabbages and Brussels-sprouts are grown.

Population and conservation: A highly successful and flourishing species, though numbers fluctuate due to parasitism of caterpillars by tiny wasps.

Egg, caterpillar and chrysalis:
EGG (*page 207*): 0·6 mm (w) × 1·4 mm (h); cylinder-shaped with ridges; pale yellow, becoming orange; laid in clusters. CATERPILLAR (*page 213*): 45 mm; dark green with black and yellow markings. The green body is heavily spotted with black on the back and has four longitudinal yellow stripes. CHRYSALIS (*page 219*): 20 mm; brown or green, speckled with black and yellow, but the colour and pattern is variable.

Foodplants: primarily wild or cultivated species of the Cruciferae family, and in particular Cabbage, though Wild Mignonette is also used.

▲ *Spring generation*   *Summer generation* ▼

UKBAP: Not listed
GB Red List: Least concern

Abundant resident

Wingspan: 38–57 mm

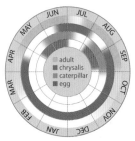

adult
chrysalis
caterpillar
egg

WHERE TO LOOK

Almost anywhere, but does not occur as far north as the Large White.

LOOK-ALIKES

Large White (*page 62*)
Green-veined White (*page 66*)
Female Orange-tip (*page 68*)
Wood White (*page 70*)
Cryptic Wood White (*page 72*)

A highly successful species that is common throughout Britain and Ireland. It is equally widespread throughout Europe, occurs as far east as Japan, and has become established in both North America and Australia.

Adult identification: Similar in appearance to the Large White (*page 62*), but usually noticeably smaller. The black on its wing tips is much less extensive than on the Large White. Females are always more heavily marked than males and have two distinct spots on the upperside of their forewings. Males have only one spot – a distinguishing feature that the male Large White lacks. Individuals from the second brood have darker markings than the first brood.

Behaviour: A common and familiar garden butterfly. The resident population is boosted every year by influxes of migrants from continental Europe. Many of these find their way into gardens where they seem to prefer to nectar on white flowers and lavenders, but lay their eggs on cultivated brassicas and Nasturtium. Like the Large White, this other 'Cabbage White' is the bane of gardeners because its caterpillars often cause considerable damage to their vegetable patches.

Breeding habitat: Almost anywhere, but gardens are particularly popular, as are fields of Oil-seed Rape.

Population and conservation: A highly successful species that continues to flourish.

Egg, caterpillar and chrysalis:
EGG (*page 207*): 0·4 mm (w) × 1·0 mm (h); bottle-shaped; straw-coloured at first, turning yellow then brownish-grey; laid singly on the underside of the leaf of a foodplant in a sheltered position.
CATERPILLAR (*page 212*): 25 mm; blue-green with a thin yellow line down the back and broken yellow lines along the sides; slightly furry.
CHRYSALIS (*page 219*): 19 mm; variable in colour, from bright green to earth-brown, depending on the background against which it forms. Supported by a silken girdle and thread and found in a variety of locations, such as on fences, walls and trees. There may also be a partial third generation.

Foodplants: cultivated brassicas and Nasturtium.

M

M

F

F

▲ *Spring generation*   *Summer generation* ▼

M

M

F

F

 ×1½ **Green-veined White** *Pieris napi*

UKBAP: Not listed
GB Red List: Least concern

Common resident

Wingspan: 40–52 mm

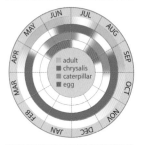

- adult
- chrysalis
- caterpillar
- egg

WHERE TO LOOK

Almost anywhere in Britain and Ireland, but absent from Shetland.

LOOK-ALIKES

Small White (*page 64*)
Large White (*page 62*)
Female Orange-tip (*page 68*)
Wood White (*page 70*)
Cryptic Wood White (*page 72*)

One of our most widespread butterflies, found throughout Britain and Ireland, apart from Shetland. It is usually the commonest white butterfly in northern Britain, and occurs at higher altitudes than the other species.

Adult identification: Though often mistaken for the Small White (*page 64*), closer inspection reveals a delicate, attractive butterfly with conspicuous dark 'veins' on the yellow underside of the hindwings. The 'veins' are actually a mottling of black scales that appear green against the yellow background. On their uppersides, females have more black markings than males. There are usually two, sometimes three generations a year. First brood butterflies are smaller than their offspring with more evident 'veins'; males may be almost white. Both sexes of the second-brood have clearer black markings on the upperside of their wings. Butterflies in Scotland (race *thomsoni*) and Ireland (race *britannica*) have stronger markings and brighter yellow underwings.

Behaviour: A wide-ranging species with a rather fluttery flight. Both sexes spend a great deal of time feeding, and males not uncommonly suck minerals from the edge of muddy puddles.

Breeding habitat: This adaptable species is found in a wide variety of habitats from hedgerows to riverbanks. Damp, lush vegetation is an essential requirement so they can often be found near damp meadows and woodland edges.

Population and conservation: One of the world's most successful butterflies, and one that continues to do well in Britain and Ireland. This species may benefit from the trend towards warmer summers.

Egg, caterpillar and chrysalis:

EGG (*page 207*): 0·4 (w) × 1·0 mm (h); elongated; pale green; laid singly.

CATERPILLAR (*page 212*): 25 mm; green; similar to Small White but lacks the yellow line along its back.

CHRYSALIS (*page 219*): 19 mm; there are two usual colour forms: green with yellow marking and pale brown with lighter marking, but combinations of these colours may also occur.

Foodplants: a range of wild crucifers, including Garlic Mustard, Charlock, Hedge Mustard and Cuckooflower.

M

F

▲ *Spring generation*   *Summer generation* ▼

M

F

M

F

Orange-tip   *Anthocharis cardamines*

UKBAP: Not listed
GB Red List: Least concern

Widespread resident

Wingspan: 40–52 mm

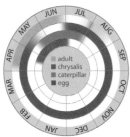

- adult
- chrysalis
- caterpillar
- egg

WHERE TO LOOK

Most easily found in countryside where a mosaic of hedgerows, small woodlands and meadows remain.

LOOK-ALIKES

Green-veined White (*page 66*)
Small White (*page 64*)
Large White (*page 62*)
Wood White (*page 70*)
Cryptic Wood White (*page 72*)

No butterfly better symbolizes the arrival of spring than this delightfully delicate species. It is extending its range northwards, and it is now well established in much of Scotland.

Adult identification: Males are unmistakable, thanks to their bright orange-tipped wings, but females are similar in appearance, shape and jizz to other whites. However, when perched they are readily identified by the beautiful green mottling of the underside of the hindwing. Irish butterflies (race *hibernica*) are slightly smaller and with a yellowish tinge.

Behaviour: Individuals in northern and southern Britain behave very differently. To the south of its range, this is a wandering species that seldom pauses for long anywhere, and strays over a wide area. In contrast, to the north of its range it apparently lives in colonies, and seldom ranges far. This may be because the foodplants are not so widely distributed.

Breeding habitat: Prefers damp, grassy habitats, including roadside verges, meadows and grassy woodland glades. In the north, it is usually found in wetter habitats where Cuckooflower grows commonly.

Population and conservation: Though this species may be extending its range northwards, its populations in the south are generally thought to be smaller than they once were. The switch from hay- to silage-making, drainage of wet meadows and the general intensification of agriculture has caused widespread loss of its favoured habitats.

Egg, caterpillar and chrysalis:

EGG (*page 207*): 0·6 mm (w) × 1·2 mm (h); bottle-shaped, long and thin; pale green when first laid, turning orange with age; laid singly on the flower-stalks of a variety of plants.

CATERPILLAR (*page 212*): 31 mm; greenish-grey on the back, fading to white on the flanks.

CHRYSALIS (*page 219*): 23 mm; initially green, with almost all turning olive-brown after about a month. Most overwinter in this form, but some do not change colour and remain green throughout the winter.

Foodplants: crucifers, most commonly Cuckooflower and Garlic Mustard, but also Charlock, Hedge Mustard, Hairy Rock-cress, Large Bitter-cress, Winter-cress and Turnip.

One of the first butterflies to look out for in the spring, when the orange of a male dashing past will catch the eye. An early season may occasionally lead to a small second brood in the summer.

Wood White *Leptidea sinapis*

UKBAP: PRIORITY
GB Red List: ENDANGERED
W&C Act: SALE PROHIBITED

Rare resident

Wingspan	Male:	42 mm
	Female:	36–48 mm

♂♀

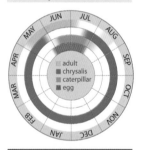

- adult
- chrysalis
- caterpillar
- egg

WHERE TO LOOK

The English strongholds are in the Midlands, Somerset and Devon. Classic sites are Oaken Wood in Surrey, Salcey Forest in Northants and Whitecross Green Wood near Oxford.

LOOK-ALIKES

Cryptic Wood White (*page 72*)
Small White (*page 64*)
Green-veined White (*page 66*)
Female Orange-tip (*page 68*)

Our rarest resident white butterfly, being found locally in England and Wales and The Burren region of Ireland.

Adult identification: A small, delicate species with a characteristic slow, fluttering flight. Their shape is distinctive, too: the wings are rather long and oval, the body long and slim. Adults only settle with their wings closed, obscuring the distinctive black dot on the leading corner of their forewing. The first generation tends to have darker markings on the underwings than the second generation. Butterflies from the Burren area in Ireland have a slightly greener underside. However, Cryptic Wood White (*page 72*) is widespread in Ireland and looks the same; a microscopic examination of the genitalia is needed to confirm identification.

Behaviour: On bright days, males fly almost continuously, slowly patrolling in search of females. Their flight is low, seldom more than a metre above the ground. Females spend most of their time feeding or resting. On hot days, the males will sip salts from the edge of puddles. Their courtship is curious with the pair sitting head-to-head; the male waves his proboscis and antennae back and forth to stimulate the female before they turn round to begin mating.

Breeding habitat: In England and Wales, usually found in woodland rides or clearings, though some colonies can be found on coastal undercliffs and disused railway lines. In Ireland, it seems to be confined to Hazel scrub in The Burren region of County Clare.

Population and conservation: This species has declined seriously in England and Wales due to loss of habitat and, in particular, the decline in coppicing and over-growth of woodland rides. If habitat is managed, and open, sunny rides maintained, colonies do much better.

Egg, caterpillar and chrysalis:

EGG (*page 207*): 0·5 mm (w) × 1·3 mm (h); bottle-shaped; pale; laid singly on the foodplant.

CATERPILLAR (*page 212*): 19 mm; green, with a dark line along the middle of the back and a yellow line along the flank.

CHRYSALIS (*page 219*): 16 mm; yellowish-green with a thin red line over the position of the emerging butterfly's antennae; formed in tussocks of grass away from the foodplant.

Foodplants: Meadow Vetchling, Bitter Vetch, Tufted Vetch and Common and Greater Bird's-foot-trefoils.

F   M

▲ *Spring generation*   *Summer generation* ▼

F   M

The spring generation is usually more numerous than the summer generation; a warm day in early June is best.

Colonies thrive in open, sunny woodland rides.

Cryptic Wood White

Leptidea juvernica

UKBAP: Not assessed
GB Red List: Not assessed

Rare resident

Wingspan: 42 mm

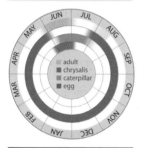

■ adult
■ chrysalis
■ caterpillar
■ egg

WHERE TO LOOK

Along the edges of rough grassland, hedgerows and road verges throughout Ireland, but not in The Burren region in County Clare, where Wood White occurs.

LOOK-ALIKES

Wood White (*page 70*)
Small White (*page 64*)
Green-veined White (*page 66*)
Female Orange-tip (*page 68*)

A rare white butterfly, restricted in the British Isles to Ireland. Although recorded since 1903 it was only recognized as a species in the late 1980s, and first found in Ireland in 2001.

Adult identification: A small, delicate butterfly, identical in appearance to Wood White (*page 70*). Cryptic Wood White can only be safely distinguished from Wood White by microscopic examination of the genitalia which differ in size and shape to the extent that it is impossible for the two species to interbreed.

Behaviour: Very similar to the Wood White, though the characteristic slow, fluttering flight appears to be a little stronger.

Breeding habitat: This species is found throughout Ireland away from The Burren area in County Clare. It breeds in more open habitats than the Wood White, including sand dunes, rough grassland, hedges and road verges, old railway lines and light scrub. Cryptic Wood White is single-brooded in Ireland, unlike on the continent, though records of the species in August may hint that a second brood occurs in some years.

Population and conservation: This species was originally thought to be *L. reali* or Réal's Wood White. Following DNA analysis, it is now known to be *L. juvernica* and given the English name Cryptic Wood White. Most of the colonies in Ireland outside The Burren have been proven to be this species. Like the Wood White, it is believed to be declining due to agricultural intensification and has been listed as a priority species in Northern Ireland.

Egg, caterpillar and chrysalis:
EGG (*page 207*): 0·5 mm (w) × 1·3 mm (h); bottle-shaped; pale; laid singly on the foodplant.
CATERPILLAR (*page 212*): 19 mm; green, with a dark line along the middle of the back and a yellow line along the flank.
CHRYSALIS (*page 219*): 16 mm; yellowish-green, with a blurred and pinker line over the position of the emerging butterfly's antennae than in Wood White; formed in tussocks of grass away from the foodplant.

Foodplants: primarily Meadow Vetchling, but also Bush Vetch (unlike Wood White) and Common Bird's-foot-trefoil.

In both species of wood white, females are slightly larger than males.

The active males rarely stop to feed; females are less active, and can often be seen egg-laying in June.

Cryptic Wood White can be found in more open habitat than Wood White, including sand dunes such as those at Murlough NNR in County Down.

Swallowtail

Papilio machaon

UKBAP: Not listed
GB Red List: Near Threatened
W&C Act: Full Protection

Localized resident

Wingspan Male: 76–83 mm
Female: 86–93 mm

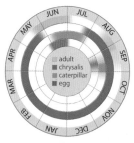

- adult
- chrysalis
- caterpillar
- egg

The only British representative of the spectacular family of swallowtail butterflies. Our resident race, *britannicus*, is restricted to the fenlands of the Norfolk Broads.

Adult identification: Unmistakable, thanks to its size, colour and shape. Occasionally, Swallowtails from continental Europe occur in southern England. These are a different race, *gorganus* (see *page 23*), and are slightly larger with paler markings. The sexes of both races look the same, except that females are usually larger than males.

Behaviour: Adults tend to feed in the morning and evening, attracted especially to Yellow Iris, thistles and Ragged-Robin. When feeding they often flap their wings to maintain their balance. Males spend much of their day on the wing: their flight is powerful, with distinctive flaps and glides. Courtship is spectacular, with both butterflies soaring high into the sky.

Breeding habitat: Our resident race is restricted to open sedge fens and reed marshes in the Norfolk Broads, where Milk-parsley grows abundantly. They may be attracted to garden flowers when these are growing nearby. Migrants from continental Europe are much more catholic in their choice of habitat and foodplants, but are only likely to be seen very occasionally in Britain.

Population and conservation: Thanks to habitat management in the Broads, this species is now thriving, especially on nature reserves. The Great Fen Project will hopefully lead to their return to one of their old haunts in fenland around The Wash. There is also a possibility that warmer summers could lead to continental Swallowtails becoming established in southern England.

Egg, caterpillar and chrysalis:

Egg (*page 208*): 1·0 mm (w) × 0·9 mm (h); spherical; shiny yellow at first, becoming dark brown with age.
Caterpillar (*page 213*): 52 mm; resembles a bird dropping at first, but the mature caterpillar is distinctive, with its green body banded with black, and each band spotted with orange.
Chrysalis (*page 224*): 28–32 mm; there are two distinct colour forms: mottled brown and yellowish-green.

Foodplant: Milk-parsley.

WHERE TO LOOK

There are a number of nature reserves within the Norfolk Broads where the habitat is managed specially for this spectacular butterfly. Well-known sites are Catfield Fen, How Hill, Strumpshaw Fen and Wheatfen.

LOOK-ALIKES

Unmistakable!

Normally easy to find in the second or third week of June, when the population is at its peak.

The British race britannicus usually has only a single brood, but in some years second-brood individuals may be seen on the Broads in August.

Green Hairstreak

Callophrys rubi

UKBAP: Not listed
GB Red List: Least concern

Widespread resident

Wingspan: 27–34 mm

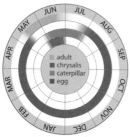

WHERE TO LOOK

This is the most widespread hairstreak in Britain and Ireland. It prefers warm, sheltered sites with plenty of scrub on chalk downland, heathland or moorland. Reliable sites include Martin Down in Hampshire and Devil's Dyke in Cambridgeshire.

LOOK-ALIKES

Small Heath (*page 156*)

Like all the hairstreaks, this species is easily overlooked, despite occurring in a wide variety of habitats. It is still widespread, but habitat destruction during recent decades has led to the loss of many colonies.

Adult identification: Unmistakable, as this is the only British butterfly with a green underside to its wings. The sexes are very similar. Their upperside is a plain and unmarked brown and they are virtually indistinguishable except that the female is very slightly larger and slightly paler than the male. The male has a light-coloured sex-brand on its forewing although this is not normally visible.

Behaviour: Territorial males have favourite perches on prominent shrubs, from which they launch periodic attacks on intruding males or chase passing females, usually returning to the same perch. When perched, always with wings closed, they are usually tame and approachable. Females are most likely to be seen when egg-laying.

Breeding habitat: Found on a wide variety of soils, and in a range of habitats including woodland rides, heathland, moorland and chalk downland. Its chief requirements are open grassland or moorland with patches of scrub.

Population and conservation: Still widespread, but many colonies have been lost through habitat destruction or deterioration; overgrazing and afforestation have led to losses in upland habitats. This species requires careful grazing and scrub management.

Egg, caterpillar and chrysalis:

EGG (*page 210*): 0·3 mm (w) × 0·65 mm (w); white.
CATERPILLAR (*page 214*): 16–18 mm; green with yellow markings, and strong indentations between the segments.
CHRYSALIS (*page 220*): 8·0–9·5 mm; brown, hairy, and formed underground, possibly in an ants' nest.

Foodplants: a wide variety, including Common Bird's-foot-trefoil and Common Rock-rose on chalk downland; Gorse and Broom on moorland, and Bilberry in Scotland.

A much overlooked species, partly because of its early flight period.

The all brown upperside is only seen in flight.

Tapping likely-looking bushes in suitable habitat in early June may flush perching males.

Typical scrub where Green Hairstreak may be found.

Brown Hairstreak

Thecla betulae

Localized resident

Wingspan Male: 36–41 mm
Female: 39–45 mm

♂♀

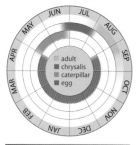

- adult
- chrysalis
- caterpillar
- egg

WHERE TO LOOK

Woodland edges with abundant Blackthorn in southern England and south-west Wales. Whitecross Green Wood near Oxford and Shipton Bellinger in Hampshire are good sites. The Burren in Co. Clare is the best location in Ireland.

LOOK-ALIKES

Black Hairstreak (*page 80*)

One of the last butterflies to appear each year and one of our rarest species, having been lost from many areas due to the loss and mechanized management of hedgerows.

Adult identification: Our largest hairstreak. Both sexes have dark chocolate-brown upperwings with orange 'tails', but the larger female also has a bright band of golden-orange across its forewings. The underside is a contrasting orange-yellow, more intense on the female, and with more of an olive tinge on the male, with white 'hairstreak' lines across both wings. If seen well, identification is easy.

Behaviour: One of our most elusive butterflies, as it spends most of its life out of sight, either high in a tree canopy or tucked away in hedgerows. Males adopt a 'master tree', normally an Ash, which stands above the surrounding tree canopy. Here they congregate, along with unmated females after they emerge. Males only rarely descend to feed, but when they do they are tame and approachable. Females are more often seen, as they disperse to lay their eggs, but they are only active on sunny days when the temperature is above 20 °C.

Breeding habitat: Usually found in hedgerows, scrub and woodland edge, with abundant Blackthorn, on heavy clay soils. Irish colonies are found on lighter, limestone soils.

Population and conservation: Hedgerow destruction and modern management practices have led to a considerable decline in the distribution of this butterfly. Annual hedge-trimming by tractor-mounted mechanical flails destroys eggs. Conservation is difficult because a single colony breeds over a wide area. Reducing the frequency of hedge-trimming and the retention of woodland is the best measure.

Egg, caterpillar and chrysalis:
EGG (*page 210*): 0·7 mm (w) × 0·6 mm (h); white, and laid singly on young twigs of its foodplant.

CATERPILLAR (*page 214*): 18 mm; pale green with yellow stripes, strongly indented between segments, turning purple before pupation.

CHRYSALIS (*page 220*): 12 mm; brown, with darker blotches; formed on the ground at the base of a clump of grass, in a crevice or on a leaf; attractive to ants, which often cover the chrysalis with soil.

Foodplant: Blackthorn.

A difficult species to see, spending much of its time high in the canopy or deep in hedgerows.

Use binoculars to scan tree-tops for males; look for females egg-laying on Blackthorn on hot August days.

Hedgerows with abundant Blackthorn are an essential requirement for the Brown Hairstreak.

Black Hairstreak

Satyrium pruni

UKBAP: Not listed
GB Red List: ENDANGERED
W&C Act: SALE PROHIBITED

Rare resident

Wingspan Male: 34–39 mm
Female: 35–40 mm

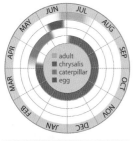

- adult
- chrysalis
- caterpillar
- egg

WHERE TO LOOK

Restricted to woodlands on heavy clay soils, between Oxford and Peterborough. Monks Wood NNR and Brampton Wood in Cambridgeshire and Glapthorn Cow Pasture in Northamptonshire are reliable sites.

LOOK-ALIKES

White-letter Hairstreak (*page 82*)
Purple Hairstreak (*page 84*)

With under 50 known colonies, all in the East Midlands, this is one of our rarest and most secretive butterflies.

Adult identification: Easily confused with White-letter (*page 82*) and Purple Hairstreaks (*page 84*) when seen from the ground. They can be difficult to identify even when settled at ground level: look for the row of black and white spots along the inner edge of the orange margin to the underside of the hindwing. The name is misleading because the uppersides of the wings are dark brown, rather than black; there are orange markings on the uppersides, which are more extensive in the female, though since they always settle with their wings closed, this is not a useful feature in the field. The 'tails' of females are slightly longer and angled very slightly upwards when compared with those of males.

Behaviour: Highly elusive, spending much of its time sitting out of sight on the top of Blackthorn bushes or Ash or Field Maple trees, feeding on aphid honeydew. When they do fly, their flight is characteristically jerky, very similar to that of Purple and White-letter Hairstreaks. They occasionally come down to the ground, attracted to the flowers of Bramble, dog-roses or Wild Privet and when feeding or basking are often tame and allow a close approach.

Breeding habitat: Typically mature and dense stands of Blackthorn in sheltered and sunny positions, but they may also occur along sheltered hedgerows or in small patches of scrub.

Population and conservation: Their population has declined steadily during the last century, mainly due to the clearance of Blackthorn. The majority of colonies are now on nature reserves where their habitat can be managed. Protective fencing may be needed to prevent deer browsing which hinders shrub re-growth.

Egg, caterpillar and chrysalis:

EGG (*page 210*): 0·8 mm (w) × 0·4 mm (h); shaped like a tiny flattened ball; usually laid on the twigs of mature Blackthorn, where they remain for nine months before hatching.
CATERPILLAR (*page 214*): 16 mm; changes colour with age, becoming bright leaf-green.
CHRYSALIS (*page 220*): 9·5 mm; attached to a twig; resembles a bird dropping.

Foodplant: Blackthorn.

Difficult to find, even at known colonies, spending much of its time out of view feeding on honeydew.

Use binoculars to scan the tops of trees and bushes during 'Wimbledon fortnight'.

Typical Black Hairstreak habitat: dense, mature stands of Blackthorn.

White-letter Hairstreak

Satyrium w-album

| UKBAP: PRIORITY |
| GB Red List: ENDANGERED |
| W&C Act: SALE PROHIBITED |

Widespread resident

♂♀ | **Wingspan** Male: 25–35 mm
Female: 26–36 mm

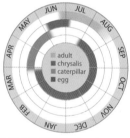

adult
chrysalis
caterpillar
egg

JUN JUL AUG SEP OCT NOV DEC JAN FEB MAR APR MAY

WHERE TO LOOK

Wherever there are elms in southern and central England. Stockbridge Down in Hampshire, Hadleigh Castle CP in Essex, Narborough Railway Line in Norfolk and Fermyn Woods in Northamptonshire have been reliable sites.

LOOK-ALIKES

Purple Hairstreak (*page 84*)
Black Hairstreak (*page 80*)

Although this elm-dependent butterfly has survived habitat loss due to Dutch Elm Disease by colonizing elm suckers and the more disease-resistant Wych Elm, there is still concern about its continuing decline.

Adult identification: Look for the distinctive white letter W on the underside. It is often very difficult to distinguish between males and females although males generally have shorter 'tails' than females. Most easily confused with the Black Hairstreak (*page 80*), but paler on the underside with a black line along the inner edge of the orange margin to the underside of the hindwing (rather than Black Hairstreak's row of dots). The upperwings are darker than the Black Hairstreak and lack orange markings, but, as it never settles with its wings open, this is invariably impossible to see.

Behaviour: Like other hairstreaks, this species spends much of its time high in the tree canopy and is easily overlooked. When it does fly, it has the erratic, spiralling flight typical of the hairstreaks. They will occasionally take nectar from nearby flowers, generally early in the morning or late in the afternoon, favouring Creeping Thistle and Bramble.

Breeding habitat: This species requires elm trees, and is usually found in sheltered hedgerows where elm suckers grow well. It can also be found on isolated, mature elm trees where these remain.

Population and conservation: Although dependent upon elms, this hairstreak has managed to overcome the problems caused by Dutch Elm Disease by breeding on elm suckers (the shoots of elm that grow from the rootstock). After a serious decline in the 1970s, it appears to have recovered, although there is still concern over the species' future as the long-term trend has been downwards.

Egg, caterpillar and chrysalis:

EGG (*page 210*): 0·8 mm (w) × 0·4 mm (h); flying-saucer shaped; laid on elm twigs.

CATERPILLAR (*page 214*): 16 mm; green, and well camouflaged on an elm leaf.

CHRYSALIS (*page 220*): 9 mm; brown and hairy, closely resembling an elm bud.

Foodplant: elms.

Easily overlooked, look for the erratic flight above the tree-tops in July.

The distinctive 'W' on the hindwing is best observed when nectaring during early morning or late afternoon.

Sheltered hedgerows with healthy elm suckers are the primary habitat.

Purple Hairstreak
Neozephyrus quercus

| UKBAP: Not listed |
| GB Red List: Least concern |
| Wildlife (NI) Order: PROTECTED |

Widespread resident

| Wingspan | Male: 33–40 mm |
| | Female: 31–38 mm |

♂♀

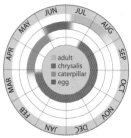

- adult
- chrysalis
- caterpillar
- egg

WHERE TO LOOK

Check suitable habitat with oak trees anywhere within range. Good sites are at Sheringham Park in Norfolk where a high wooden gazebo allows observation at canopy level, Alner's Gorse in Dorset and Bookham Common in Surrey.

LOOK-ALIKES

White-letter Hairstreak (*page 82*)
Black Hairstreak (*page 80*)

This beautiful butterfly is surprisingly widespread and often quite numerous. Although it is the commonest British hairstreak, it is easily overlooked.

Adult identification: No other butterfly of this size shares the same attractive colouring. A freshly-emerged male's black-edged wings are sheened with purple. Females are not so bright but have a purple patch on each forewing. The underwings of both sexes are similar, with prominent white lines on a greyish background, and orange-yellow spots near the corner of the hindwing.

Behaviour: Lives in self-contained colonies, always on oak trees. They seldom take flight, except on sunny days, when they can be seen flying around the tree-tops, but only occasionally descending to lower branches or flowers. Individuals become active in the late afternoon and early evening on bright, sunny days. When seen in flight from below, they appear silver. Unlike our other hairstreaks, they bask with their wings open.

Breeding habitat: Oak trees in mature woodlands, parklands and hedgerows; sometimes in scrub oak on heathland. Even single, isolated trees may support a colony.

Population and conservation: Recent increases in range indicate a healthy population, even though many colonies were lost during the last century. They are found throughout southern England and the Midlands, extending northwards to south-west Scotland. The future looks bright for this species in England and Wales, if not in Ireland, where it has always been very rare.

Egg, caterpillar and chrysalis:
EGG (*page 210*): 0·8 mm (w) × 0·5 mm (h); white; laid in ones or twos on the tips of oak branches, close to the following year's buds.
CATERPILLAR (*page 214*): 16 mm; greenish-brown, well camouflaged as the colour of oak buds, and lives in a silken cocoon at the base of a bud.
CHRYSALIS (*page 220*): 10 mm; dark reddish-brown, formed at ground level and sometimes found in ants' nests.

Foodplant: oaks.

Search the canopy with binoculars in late afternoon or early evening on bright sunny days in July and August.

You may need to watch an oak tree patiently for up to ten minutes to be sure of detecting movement between the branches high up in and around the canopy.

Holly Blue

Celastrina argiolus

UKBAP: Not listed	
GB Red List: Least concern	
Wildlife (NI) Order: PROTECTED	

Common resident

Wingspan:	26–34 mm

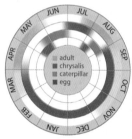

- adult
- chrysalis
- caterpillar
- egg

WHERE TO LOOK

Churchyards, with their abundance of Holly and Ivy, are often good places to look, but large, sheltered gardens also attract this butterfly.

LOOK-ALIKES

Small Blue (*page 88*)
Common Blue (*page 96*)

The first of the blue butterflies on the wing, this is a widespread species which is extending its range, but one whose numbers fluctuate wildly from year to year.

Adult identification: Habitat and timing are good clues to identifying this species. A blue butterfly, seen in April flying around Holly, is almost certainly a Holly Blue, but confusion is possible later in the year when Common Blues (*page 96*) are on the wing. A good view of the underside will confirm the identification, however, for the Holly Blue has a distinctive pale blue underwing spotted lightly with black and silver, but with no trace of orange. In addition, the upperwings of the female have distinctive black margins.

Behaviour: Wandering individuals can often be seen be seen moving along hedgerows or through sheltered gardens, typically flying much higher than any of the other blues. They will often settle high on sunlit conifers and drink aphid honeydew. In dry summers, the males may come down to take salts from muddy puddles. They typically perch with their wings closed, although they do open them, particularly in weak sunshine.

Breeding habitat: A wide variety of habitats are used, ranging from hedgerows and woodland rides to gardens and urban parks.

Population and conservation: Populations typically rise for a few years and then peak before crashing, probably due to the effects of depredation by the parasitic ichneumon wasp *Listrodomus nycthemerus*. However, the Holly Blue is extending its range northwards, and is flourishing in Britain (although it is still more local in Ireland). It can be encouraged to visit gardens by planting Holly and Ivy in sunny positions and leaving them to produce fruit.

Egg, caterpillar and chrysalis:
EGG (*page 208*): 0·7 mm (w) × 0·4 mm (h); resembles a tiny white disc; and laid directly onto the foodplant.
CATERPILLAR (*page 215*): 15 mm; base colour normally green, with a whitish line along either side, but markings vary considerably.
CHRYSALIS (*page 221*): 8–9 mm; sepia, speckled with brown, but very rarely found in the wild.

Foodplants: Holly (first brood) and Ivy (second brood).

The first brood is generally more conspicuous than the second, possibly because the trees have less foliage.

Females have distinctive black margins to the upperwings; these markings are usually broader in the second brood (below).

| UKBAP: Priority |
| GB Red List: Near Threatened |
| W&C Act: Sale Prohibited |
| Wildlife (NI) Order: Protected |

Declining resident

Wingspan: 18–25 mm

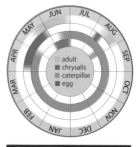

WHERE TO LOOK

Though it occurs from Caithness to Dorset, its strongholds are the Cotswolds and downland on Salisbury Plain.

LOOK-ALIKES

Holly Blue (*page 86*)
Common Blue (*page 96*)

Our smallest butterfly, which is patchily distributed throughout Britain and Ireland and is declining in most areas.

Adult identification: Readily identified with practice thanks to its small size, dainty appearance and rounded wings with silvery-blue undersides. These are dotted with black, lacking the orange found on most blues, and resemble a tiny Holly Blue (*page 86*). Though the underside of both sexes is similar, the female lacks any hint of blue in her upperwings, while the male shows a distinct scatter of blue scales at the base of the wings. The flight is weak and fluttery.

Behaviour: A colonial species that is usually highly sedentary, but does occasionally disperse to new sites. Males can typically be found basking together in a sheltered south-facing site, usually at the base of a hill, quarry slope or railway embankment. Here they spend most of the day perched up to a metre or so above the ground, and spaced up to a couple of metres apart, with wings held partially open towards the sun. Any passing female is quickly courted and mated by a waiting male; she then spends her time on patches of Kidney Vetch, where she not only rests and feeds, but also lays her eggs.

Breeding habitat: This species favours sheltered grassland, usually on chalk or limestone, where Kidney Vetch grows in abundance and there is a mixture of short turf and taller, scrubby vegetation.

Population and conservation: Its special requirements of shelter and abundant Kidney Vetch limit the number of sites where this species can be found. Habitat loss during the past century has led to the extinction of many colonies. The increasing isolation of many populations and the lack of suitable site management are major threats to its survival, and explains why this species is in worrying decline.

Egg, caterpillar and chrysalis:

EGG (*page 208*): 0·45 mm (w) × 0·2 mm (h); tiny and disc-shaped; white; laid within the flower-head of the foodplant. CATERPILLAR (*page 215*): 9·5 mm; pale yellow, with a darker line down the back, and a whitish line along each side. CHRYSALIS (*page 221*): 8 mm; pale sepia with brown dots.

Foodplant: Kidney Vetch.

The underside lacks orange and resembles that of a tiny Holly Blue.

M

M

Look for open-winged males perched in scrub about a metre off the ground.

F

F

This is a spring butterfly, best looked for in early June when numbers peak.

Chalk grassland with scrub and abundant Kidney Vetch are required.

UKBAP: Not listed
GB Red List: Least concern
Widespread resident

Wingspan: 25–31 mm

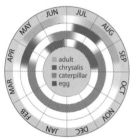

adult
chrysalis
caterpillar
egg

WHERE TO LOOK

Though widespread in south-eastern England, the most reliable sites to see this species are on chalk downland in the southern counties and the Cotswolds.

LOOK-ALIKES

Common Blue (*page 96*)
Northern Brown Argus
(*page 92*)
Adonis Blue (*page 98*)
Chalkhill Blue (*page 100*)

Confusingly, this brown butterfly is one of the blues. It is found on many different open habitats but is most common on chalk and limestone grassland.

Adult identification: Closely resembles the brown form of the female Common Blue (*page 96*), although is noticeably smaller. The most reliable characteristic is the silvery appearance of both sexes when in flight. This is caused by reflection of light from the underwings. When the butterfly is basking with wings open, one consistent feature to look for is a complete absence of blue scales on the upperwings (female Common Blues usually show a hint of blue). Unlike Common, Adonis (*page 98*) and Chalkhill (*page 100*) Blues, the underside of the forewing lacks spots close to the body.

Behaviour: A low-flying species, stopping frequently to sip nectar from a flower, or to bask in the sun. Males often land on the ground. It lives in colonies, although most are fairly small so you seldom see them in a crowd. At first light, adults bask together in the sun, wings stretched wide to absorb the maximum energy. As with other blues, the caterpillars have a strong relationship with ants.

Breeding habitat: Mostly found on chalk and limestone grassland, but adaptable and may also occur in a wide variety of other situations, including heathland, coastal dunes, woodland clearings and road verges.

Population and conservation: After a century of slow decline due to habitat loss, there was a resurgence in numbers in the 1990s, helped by a series of warmer summers and by the extra habitat offered by fields that were set aside from cultivation for a few years. The population has now stabilized and there has been a gradual spread into South Yorkshire and the Peak District.

Egg, caterpillar and chrysalis:

Egg (*page 208*): 0·5 mm (w) × 0·3 mm (h); a pale, blue-green disc, becoming pearl-white before hatching; laid on the underside of leaves of the foodplant.

Caterpillar (*page 215*): 11 mm; green, with a purplish-green stripe along its back and along the sides.

Chrysalis (*page 221*): 8 mm; pale pinkish-green or olive-yellow; formed on the ground at the base of the foodplant.

Foodplants: usually Common Rock-rose, though various other plants are also used, especially species of crane's-bill.

Flies close to the ground, frequently pausing to nectar.

Occasionally, forewing spots show white haloes.

Double-brooded with a prolonged emergence and so can be encountered all summer long.

Forewing spot close to the body

No forewing spot

Unbroken white fringe
Common Blue

Broken white fringe
Adonis Blue

Chalkhill Blue

Relatively broad black line
Silver-studded Blue

Thin black line
Brown Argus

The Brown Argus can be distinguished by the lack of a forewing spot close to the body.

Chalk grassland is the primary habitat.

Northern Brown Argus *Aricia artaxerxes*

Localized resident

Wingspan: 26–35 mm

As its name suggests, this is a northern species, and is widespread in Scandinavia. It can be found in small but scattered colonies in Scotland and Northern England.

Adult identification: Very closely related to the Brown Argus (*page 90*), from which those found in Scotland can easily be distinguished by having a white spot on the upperside of each forewing and fainter black spots on their undersides. The few colonies south of the border belong to a separate race, *salmacis*, which has similar genetic characteristics to their Scottish relatives *artaxerxes* but lack the white spots. Northern Brown Argus and Brown Argus are most reliably separated by range although recent genetic studies have discovered that these species appear to overlap in some locations.

Behaviour: A highly sedentary species, invariably found in small colonies of fewer than 200 adults. Its general behaviour is very similar to that of its southern counterpart, and there is a similar association with ants. It is single-brooded, unlike the Brown Argus which usually has two broods (although some Brown Argus colonies in the Peak District and North Wales are single-brooded).

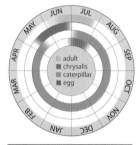

Breeding habitat: Sheltered and well-drained hillsides, usually on limestone, where its foodplant, Common Rock-rose, flourishes. In Scotland, it may also occur on acidic soils provided that rock-roses can grow there. It favours areas of bare ground within its habitat.

Population and conservation: This species has declined in recent years in northern England, but is still relatively plentiful within its Scottish range. Fragmentation and destruction of habitat has, however, led to the loss of many colonies. It requires light grazing by rabbits, sheep or cattle, preferably in autumn and winter, to create suitable conditions, and responds quickly to habitat management.

WHERE TO LOOK

Smardale Gill in Cumbria and Bishop Middleham Quarry in Co. Durham are well-known English sites. In Scotland, it is found at St Abb's Head in Berwickshire and many other places in north Tayside and Perthshire.

LOOK-ALIKES

Brown Argus (*page 90*)
Common Blue (*page 96*)

Egg, caterpillar and chrysalis:

EGG (*page 208*): 0·6 mm (w) × 0·3 mm (h); a pale, blue-green disc laid on the upperside of leaves (unlike Brown Argus).

CATERPILLAR (*page 215*): 12 mm; similar to Brown Argus: light-green, with a purplish stripe along the back and lighter stripes along each side.

CHRYSALIS (*page 221*): 8·5 mm; sandy green; formed on the ground.

Foodplant: Common Rock-rose.

M

M

F

F

▲ *The race* artaxerxes *found in Scotland.*

The race salmacis *found in northern England.* ▼

M

M

The extent of orange markings is variable in the race salmacis; *some, like the male above, may also have a forewing spot that is partially white.*

M

Flight period varies considerably each year and from colony to colony. Most southern colonies peak in numbers from late June to early July, but often weeks later in northern Scotland.

F

F

Silver-studded Blue

Plebeius argus

UKBAP: Priority
GB Red List: Vulnerable
W&C Act: Sale Prohibited

Localized resident

♂♀ **Wingspan** Male: 26–32 mm
Female: 25–31 mm

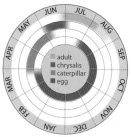

- adult
- chrysalis
- caterpillar
- egg

WHERE TO LOOK

Many lowland heaths in Hampshire and Dorset have thriving colonies. Other well-known sites include Penhale Dunes in Cornwall, on the Great Orme in North Wales, the Isle of Portland in Dorset and Kelling Heath in Norfolk.

LOOK-ALIKES

Common Blue (*page 96*)

A localized butterfly of heathland. Many colonies have been lost during the last century, but it can still be abundant.

Adult identification: Extremely variable species. The male is best told from the similar Common Blue (*page 96*) by the thick black borders to both its underwing and upperwing. Like many of the other blues, females have upperwings which are mainly brown, but may show some blue **Fb**. In both sexes, the outer edge of the underside of the hindwings has a series of metallic-blue-centred spots – hence the butterfly's name, though 'silver' is rather a misnomer. A separate race (*caernensis*) is found on the Great Orme in North Wales.

Behaviour: The flight is usually slow, fluttering and ground-hugging. Individuals rarely travel more than 20 m from where they emerged. Males are very active on sunny days, patrolling continuously in search of unmated females. Communal roosting involving sometimes hundreds of individuals is normal. This butterfly has a close relationship with ants, which attend the caterpillars, licking their sugar-rich secretions in return.

Breeding habitat: Lowland heathland is the typical habitat, but this species also occurs on limestone grasslands and sand dunes. Short vegetation, and a thriving black ant population are the main requirements.

Population and conservation: Although colonies of hundreds or even thousands of individuals can still be found, the widespread fragmentation and loss of lowland heathland has led to the extinction of many populations. Many downland colonies were also lost in the 1950s due to myxomatosis reducing the population of grazing rabbits. Habitat management is essential for survival of the remaining colonies, either grazing or periodic burning of small patches.

Egg, caterpillar and chrysalis:
Egg (*page 208*): 0·6 mm (w) × 0·3 mm (h); disc-like; white; usually laid near nests of the black ants *Lasius niger* or *L. alienus*.
Caterpillar (*page 215*): 13 mm; varies from bright pale-green to brown with a blackish stripe along the back and a white stripe along each side.
Chrysalis (*page 221*): 8–9 mm; green; formed underground in an ants' nest or carried there by ants after they have been formed.

Foodplants: include Gorse, Heather, Bell Heather, Cross-leaved Heath, Common Bird's-foot-trefoil, Horseshoe Vetch and Common Rock-rose.

The thick black border on the upperside of both wings distinguishes the male from other blues.

Females are reminiscent of a faded Brown Argus (page 90) but the relatively thick black line along the inside of the white fringe on the underside rules out that species.

A colonial species with a ground-hugging flight; peak numbers occur in mid-July.

F *caernensis (Great Orme only): smaller and with the females mainly blue in colour.*

The caernensis *race emerges in late June, a fortnight earlier than most other colonies.*

Lowland heath is the typical habitat.

Common Blue   *Polyommatus icarus*

UKBAP: Not listed
GB Red List: Least concern

Widespread resident

Wingspan: 29–38 mm

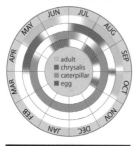

WHERE TO LOOK

Almost anywhere in Britain and Ireland, below 500 m. Look for them early or late in the day, when individuals can be highly approachable as they bask in weak sunshine with wings held flat.

LOOK-ALIKES

Adonis Blue (*page 98*)
Silver-studded Blue (*page 94*)
Chalkhill Blue (*page 100*)
Brown Argus (*page 90*)
Northern Brown Argus (*page 92*)

By far our most widespread blue butterfly, which is still common throughout much of Britain and Ireland.

Adult identification: The male is a brilliant, eye-catching blue. Females are usually brown, with a touch of deep violet-blue near the wing-base **Fn**, which sometimes spreads over most of the upperwing **Fb**. Their wing margins are edged with orange spots. In Ireland and north-west Scotland, females are more often of the blue form, *mariscolore*, than they are of the usual brown form. Both forms have orange marks on the edges of their underwings. Like the Adonis (*page 98*) and Chalkhill (*page 100*) Blues, considerable variations occur in underwing markings (see *page 36*), although less frequently. Very occasionally, the forewing spot close to the body is absent.

Behaviour: Lives in discrete colonies, though individuals will wander some distance and are able to colonize new areas rapidly. Males are territorial and will chase away rival males, or other butterflies (*e.g.* Small Coppers). Flight is typically short but rapid as the butterfly moves from one flower to the next.

Breeding habitat: Its wide distribution reflects a catholic taste in habitat, as it can be found almost anywhere its foodplants grow. It favours sunny, sheltered areas and may be found on downland, road verges, old quarries, golf courses, woodland clearings and in rural gardens.

Population and conservation: Although this is a robust and successful species, it is vulnerable to changes in land use and loss of habitat. In the south of England, its second and third broods (if there is one) can be badly affected by drought, which reduces numbers the following year. Because it occurs in many small colonies across Britain and Ireland, this species is a good indicator of biodiversity in the wider countryside, and its continued monitoring is therefore particularly important.

Egg, caterpillar and chrysalis:
EGG (*page 208*): 0·5 mm (w) × 0·2 mm (h); white, laid on tiny, tender leaves of its foodplant.
CATERPILLAR (*page 215*): 13 mm; green body, with a dark-green line along the back and greenish-white lines along the sides.
CHRYSALIS (*page 221*): 9–10 mm; green; attractive to ants due to its sugary secretions.

Foodplants: usually Common Bird's-foot-trefoil, although other trefoils, Common Restharrow, Black Medick and White Clover are sometimes used.

Told from the similar Adonis Blue (page 98) by the unbroken white margins to the wings.

M

M

The territorial males catch the eye as they chase away rivals.

Fn

Differs from Brown Argus (page 90) and Silver-studded Blue (page 94) in having a spot on the underside of the forewing, near the body.

Fb

F

F *mariscolore*

Get close to basking indivduals early in the day.

Adonis Blue

Polyommatus bellargus

A beautiful blue butterfly that has declined in numbers due to the loss of short-grazed turf, but can still be abundant on the chalk downlands of southern England.

UKBAP: Not listed
GB Red List: Near Threatened
W&C Act: Sale Prohibited

Localized resident

Wingspan: 30–40 mm

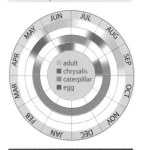

adult
chrysalis
caterpillar
egg

WHERE TO LOOK

On the chalk downlands of southern England. Classic sites include Denbies Hillside in Surrey, Martin Down in Hampshire, Mill Hill at Shoreham in West Sussex, Fontmell Down, in Dorset and Compton Bay on the Isle of Wight.

LOOK-ALIKES

Common Blue (*page 96*)
Chalkhill Blue (*page 100*)
Brown Argus (*page 90*)

Adult identification: This is the most brightly coloured of our blues, most males being a brilliant, unmistakable sky blue. The colour does vary considerably, however, some individuals appearing turquoise or even violet. They often fly alongside Common Blues (*page 96*) and may be hard to separate, particularly when they have lost some of their wing scales. Both sexes have diagnostic fine black veins that cross the outer white fringes of their wings. Females are usually brown (although bluish females are common on some sites) and look very similar to female Chalkhill Blues (*page 100*).

Behaviour: This attractive butterfly lives in highly sedentary colonies. The brilliant males are far more conspicuous than the females as they patrol slowly, just above the ground, in their quest for virgin females. Like several of the other blues, this species has a close and intriguing relationship with ants (either the black ant *Lasius alienus* or the red ant *Myrmica sabuleti*).

Breeding habitat: Unimproved and unfertilized close-cropped dry chalk or limestone grassland turf on south-facing slopes with an abundance of Horseshoe Vetch.

Population and conservation: Though this species' distribution is highly restricted, it can be abundant on some sites. Following previous declines, there has been a recovery in numbers in recent years, almost certainly due to a post-myxomatosis resurgence in rabbit populations, and better habitat management. Global warming may well lead to a continued population increase if our summers do not become too dry for Horseshoe Vetch to thrive.

Egg, caterpillar and chrysalis:

Egg (*page 208*): 0·5 mm (w) × 0·3 mm (h); laid singly.
Caterpillar (*page 215*): 15 mm; dark green with yellow stripes; invariably attended by ants.
Chrysalis (*page 221*): 11 mm; formed underground in association with ants.

Foodplant: Horseshoe Vetch.

The black veins that cross the white outer margins to the wings are diagnostic.

M

M

Brilliant blue males are conspicuous as they patrol slowly, just above the ground.

Females are told from the similar Chalkhill Blue (page 100) by the colour of the pale crescents below the orange and black 'spots' on the upperside along the border of the hindwing:

F

F

blue in Adonis Blue,

white in Chalkhill Blue.

The population is double-brooded, peaking at the end of May and at the end of August.

The sedentary colonies need Horseshoe Vetch in abundance on south-facing chalk grassland.

| UKBAP: Not listed |
| GB Red List: NEAR THREATENED |
| W&C Act: SALE PROHIBITED |

Localized resident

Wingspan: 33–40 mm

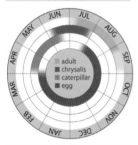

- adult
- chrysalis
- caterpillar
- egg

WHERE TO LOOK

There are many colonies in southern and south-east England, including on the North and South Downs, the Chilterns and the Cotswolds, and the Hampshire, Wiltshire and Dorset Downs.

LOOK-ALIKES

Adonis Blue (*page 98*)
Common Blue (*page 96*)
Brown Argus (*page 90*)

The aptly named Chalkhill Blue favours chalk downland. It is common where unimproved chalk downland remains, but has suffered from widespread ploughing of the downs.

Adult identification: This species is readily identified by the male's pale, almost silvery wings, quite unlike any of our other blues. The female is dark brown, and easily confused with the slightly smaller Adonis Blue (*page 98*). The sub-marginal spots on the upperside of the hindwings have white scaling near the wing edges, whereas those of Adonis Blues have blue scaling. These scales may be lost due to wear and then it is impossible to see the difference. Many colour variations occur, including blue forms of the female.

Behaviour: On sunny days, males flutter continuously over the turf searching for females. The latter, in contrast, seldom fly far except to feed or lay eggs. Feeding adults will visit a wide variety of flowers, but they are particularly fond of scabiouses, knapweeds and Kidney Vetch. In the evening, the adults roost on tall grass stems, usually at the base of a slope.

Breeding habitat: As the name suggests, this species requires unimproved and unfertilized grassland on chalk and limestone hills where its foodplant, Horseshoe Vetch, grows. Autumn or winter grazing by sheep or cattle creates the ideal sward.

Population and conservation: The ploughing and so-called 'improvement' of grassland on many of our southern downs has led to the loss of numerous colonies. The key to their conservation is grazing to prevent the foodplant being overgrown. Numbers rise during warm summers and, long-term, the population has shown a slight increase.

Egg, caterpillar and chrysalis:

EGG (*page 208*): 0·5 mm (w) × 0·3 mm (h); shell robust and sculptured; initially whitish, changing through grey to a lilac tinge; laid on or near the foodplant.

CATERPILLAR (*page 215*): 16 mm; bright green with yellow bands along the back and sides.

CHRYSALIS (*page 221*): 12 mm; ochreous yellow-green; formed on the ground under the foodplant, and attended and generally buried by ants.

Foodplant: Horseshoe Vetch.

In mid-August hundreds of Chalkhill Blues may be seen flying together.

Males are active and easy to see; females seldom fly, staying low in the vegetation.

Chalkhill Blue requires natural grassland on chalk and limestone where Horseshoe Vetch grows.

UKBAP: PRIORITY
GB Red List:
CRITICALLY ENDANGERED
W&C Act: FULL PROTECTION
EU Habs Dir: (ANN IV)
Bern Convention: (APP II)

Re-established resident

♂♀ **Wingspan** Male: 38–48mm
Female: 42–52mm

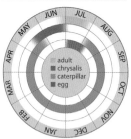

adult
chrysalis
caterpillar
egg

WHERE TO LOOK

There is an open-access site at Collard Hill in Somerset. Nearby, Green Down can be accessed as part of an organized visit.

LOOK-ALIKES

Chalkhill Blue (*page 100*)
Common Blue (*page 96*)
Adonis Blue (*page 98*)

Extinct as a native butterfly in 1979, the Large Blue has since been successfully reintroduced to a number of sites in Somerset and south-west England.

Adult identification: Its name is misleading, for though it is the largest of our blue butterflies, its size is variable, and many individuals are smaller than the Chalkhill Blue (*page 100*). Both sexes have black-edged, blue wings, with distinctive black spotting on the forewings, although the larger female is generally more heavily marked than the male. The black spots on the upperside are unique among British blues, and are the diagnostic field mark.

Behaviour: Adult males tend to be most active on sunny mornings, patrolling their breeding grounds. On hot afternoons they roost in the shade, usually emerging later to take nectar from Wild Thyme. The lifespan is about five days. The most extraordinary feature of the Large Blue's life-cycle is its dependence on one species of red ant, *Myrmica sabuleti*. These ants take the caterpillars into their nests, which then feast on the host ants' grubs. The caterpillars hibernate in the nest, and pupate the following May.

Breeding habitat: This species, and its vital red ant host, requires well-drained, unimproved grassland, closely cropped by rabbits, sheep, cattle or ponies. Historically, the preferred habitat was well-drained acidic grassland around the coast of Devon and Cornwall and, inland, warm, south-facing slopes of limestone grassland, though sites on clay soils with well-drained mounds or outcrops were also used.

Population and conservation: Reintroduction of Swedish butterflies to specially prepared sites in southern England started in 1983. The work is now co-ordinated by Butterfly Conservation in partnership with a number of conservation bodies. As a result, the species is firmly re-established at several sites. However, the sites depend on continuing management and drought is a potential problem.

Egg, caterpillar and chrysalis:

EGG (*page 208*): 0·5 (w) × 0·3 mm (h); white; laid on flowers of the foodplant.
CATERPILLAR (*page 215*): 15 mm; pale; stout-bodied, resembling an ant grub.
CHRYSALIS (*page 221*): 13 mm; sepia-brown; formed within the nests of ants.

Foodplant: Wild Thyme.

The black spots on the upperwing are unique among British blues.

Sunny mornings in early July are best for viewing this delightful butterfly.

Although well-drained unimproved grassland is widespread, it must host the red ant Myrmica sabuleti for it to be suitable for the Large Blue.

Small Copper *Lycaena phlaeas*

| UKBAP: Not listed |
| GB Red List: Least concern |

Common resident

Wingspan Male: 26–36 mm
Female: 30–40 mm

♂♀

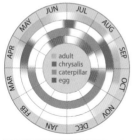

adult
chrysalis
caterpillar
egg

WHERE TO LOOK

Almost anywhere, but look for it particularly on waste ground or marginal land where sorrels flourish.

LOOK-ALIKES

Small fritillaries (*pages 108–117*)
Small Heath (*page 156*)

A common and widespread species, which underwent a major decline in abundance during the 20th century.

Adult identification: Readily identified by its brightly burnished copper forewings, with black margins and spots. The hindwings are dark with black-spotted copper margins. No other British butterfly shares the same colouring. The female is larger than the male and has slightly more rounded forewings. This species is prone to variation (see *page 37*), and a blue-spotted form called *caeruleopunctata* is often found, particularly in Scotland. Very occasionally, there is an albino aberrant with the copper colour replaced by white. Irish butterflies are of the race *hibernica* that has a slightly broader orange band on its hindwings.

Behaviour: Males are highly territorial, attacking with pugnacious enthusiasm any insect that comes close. Their flight is both fast and direct. After each quick sortie, the male usually returns to his perch, typically on a flower-head where there is good all-round visibility. They are highly active, fidgeting even when feeding.

Breeding habitat: This butterfly's widespread distribution reflects its use of a variety of habitats, ranging from heathland and unimproved grassland to woodland clearings. It is often found on waste ground, in churchyards and occasionally in gardens, and is particularly fond of warm and dry situations.

Population and conservation: There are usually two, sometimes three, and possibly four generations a year. Population declines have been linked to agricultural intensification, which leads to lush, grass-dominated swards which do not support its foodplants. Much still needs to be discovered about the ecology of this species, but it is known to suffer badly during cool, wet summers.

Egg, caterpillar and chrysalis:

EGG (*page 210*): 0·6 mm (w) × 0·3 mm (h); white, turning grey; laid singly.

CATERPILLAR (*page 215*): 16 mm; green, often with pinkish lines along its back and sides.

CHRYSALIS (*page 221*): 10·5 mm; pinkish-brown; surprisingly little is known about this stage of the life-cycle, since it is rarely found in the wild: it may be tended by ants amongst leaf-litter.

Foodplants: Common Sorrel and Sheep's Sorrel.

Easy to find on waste ground and anywhere the foodplant is plentiful.

Can be seen from early May through to mid-October.

Typical Small Copper habitat.

Duke of Burgundy

Hamearis lucina

UKBAP: PRIORITY
GB Red List: ENDANGERED
W&C Act: SALE PROHIBITED

Localized resident

♂♀ **Wingspan** Male: 29–32 mm
Female: 31–34 mm

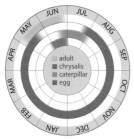

WHERE TO LOOK

Limestone grasslands in the Cotswolds, and the chalk downs of Wiltshire, Hampshire and Sussex. Reliable sites include Martin Down and Noar Hill, in Hampshire, and Totternhoe Quarry and Bison Hill in Bedfordshire.

LOOK-ALIKES

Small fritillaries (*pages 108–117*)
Chequered Skipper (*page 52*)

An attractive and highly localized spring-flying butterfly with a fritillary-like appearance, which has suffered a widespread decline in recent decades .

Adult identification: Similar to the 'small' fritillaries (*pages 108–117*), but readily identified by the two parallel bands of white spots on its underwing and the white spots along the fringes of both the forewing and hindwing. Confusion with the Chequered Skipper (*page 52*) is also possible, but the ranges of the two do not overlap in Britain.

Behaviour: This species lives in small, compact colonies. It is one of the most pugnacious of butterflies, territorial males being most conspicuous as they defend their chosen bush or grass tussock, with the resulting fights leading to spectacular aerial encounters. Resting males sit with their wings half-open. Females are much more elusive, spending most of the time resting, or flying low looking for egg-laying sites.

Breeding habitat: Two types of habitat are favoured: chalk or limestone grassland which has shelter from scrub or a hillside; or clearings in areas of ancient woodland. It prefers its foodplants to be growing amongst tussocky vegetation, and on downland it is usually found on north-facing or west-facing slopes.

Population and conservation: There has been an alarming decline in the number of colonies and overall population of this species in recent decades, and the remaining colonies are now scattered and highly localized. The decline is largely due to the intensification of agriculture on its favoured downland sites, and the cessation of coppicing in old woodlands. The resurgence of rabbits following myxomatosis has also created a problem, as they crop the sward tightly, and destroy suitable foodplants.

Egg, caterpillar and chrysalis:

EGG (*page 208*): 0·6 mm (w) × 0·6 mm (h); spherical, flattened at the base; turns pale green; laid in small groups on the foodplant.

CATERPILLAR (*page 215*): 16 mm; dark brown, short and hairy.

CHRYSALIS (*page 220*): 9 mm; pale cream with a pinkish tinge and dark brown spots and covered in fine hairs; formed on or close to the ground.

Foodplants: Primrose or Cowslip.

The territorial males are active and conspicuous, often pausing to rest with wings half-open.

Underside similar to a fritillary, but the two parallel bands of white spots on the hindwing are diagnostic.

Sheltered chalk grassland with plenty of Cowslips is ideal habitat for the Duke of Burgundy.

× 1½ **Heath Fritillary** *Melitaea athalia*

Endangered resident

Wingspan Male: 39–44 mm
Female: 42–47 mm

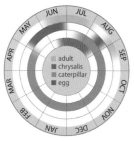

adult
chrysalis
caterpillar
egg

WHERE TO LOOK
Good places are East Blean Wood, near Canterbury in Kent, and Hockley Woods near Southend-on-Sea in Essex. On Exmoor, search for it on the south-facing slopes of sheltered valleys.

LOOK-ALIKES
Marsh Fritillary (*page 110*)
Both pearl-bordered fritillaries (*pages 114–117*)

Though one of our rarest and most localized species, this sedentary butterfly has been saved from the brink of extinction in England.

Adult identification: One of our smallest fritillaries, which can be readily recognized by its generally dark colouring – although the larger female is usually slightly paler than the male.
In Britain, it is most likely to be confused with the larger and brighter Marsh Fritillary (*page 110*) and the two species of pearl-bordered fritillary (*pages 114–117*), both of which show seven silver pearls (not six, like this species) along the borders of the underside of each hindwing. Its restricted range and sedentary nature rules out any natural occurrence away from the few known colonies.

Behaviour: Few British butterflies are more dependent on the sun than this species. On warm, sunny days, the males spend much of their time on the wing, flying with short flicks and flat-winged glides low to the ground. The inconspicuous females spend most of their short lives (5–10 days) basking, or hidden in vegetation.

Breeding habitat: Three different types of habitat are used. In Kent and Essex, there are colonies in coppiced woodland on acid soils. On Exmoor, it favours sheltered valleys. In Devon and Cornwall there are a few colonies in abandoned hay meadows.

Population and conservation: The precise habitat requirements of this specialized, warmth-loving species are now well-known, and the colonies in Essex and Kent are managed by regular coppicing, and those in the West Country by regular ground clearance to prevent overgrowth and encourage warm, sunny breeding conditions. Its future in Britain depends upon continuing, careful habitat management.

Egg, caterpillar and chrysalis:
EGG (*page 209*): 0.4 mm (w) × 0.6 mm (h); ribbed and thimble-shaped; pale-green, turning lemon-yellow; invariably laid in large batches on the undersides of leaves close to the foodplant.
CATERPILLAR (*page 216*): 22–25 mm; black, with greyish-white spots and yellow-orange spines.
CHRYSALIS (*page 222*): 12.5 mm; white, mottled with brown and black; usually found in a dead leaf close to the ground.

Foodplants: usually Common Cow-wheat, but Foxglove (Exmoor) or Ribwort Plantain and Germander Speedwell (Devon and Cornwall).

M

F

Males and females often bask together.

M

M

F

Pale individuals can resemble
Marsh Fritillary (page 110).

Sunny, warm days are essential to see this species on the wing; it seldom flies if the temperature is below 18°C.

Coppiced woodland with Common Cow-wheat is the very specific habitat used in eastern England.

The colonies in the south-west usually emerge around the end of May,
sometimes a fortnight earlier than those in Kent and Essex.

Marsh Fritillary

Euphydryas aurinia

♂♀

Wingspan   Male: 30–42 mm

Female: 40–50 mm

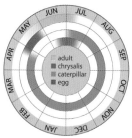

- adult
- chrysalis
- caterpillar
- egg

A beautiful but scarce and localized colonial butterfly that declined severely during the 20th century.

Adult identification: Despite being highly variable in its markings and colouration, with different colonies having their own characteristics (the Irish race *hibernica* is more richly-coloured), this species is only likely to be confused with the Heath Fritillary (*page 108*). The most obvious differences are the Marsh Fritillary's upperwing pattern, which is brighter and more contrasting; the hindwing underside which is more orange than pale; and the slightly concave front edge of the forewing. Females are larger and paler than the males.

Behaviour: Rather slow-flying in comparison with other fritillaries, keeping low to the ground. Adults rarely fly more than 100 m from where they emerged. Females are mated soon after emergence, and are so full of eggs that they crawl in the vegetation and can only fly short distances. Once their eggs have been laid, they will fly longer distances from flower to flower.

Breeding habitat: The name Marsh Fritillary is misleading, for though it favours damp, tussocky grassland where its foodplant grows, it can also be found in woodland clearings or other grasslands. During the last century, this species colonized chalk and limestone downland in the Cotswolds, Dorset and Wiltshire, as well as damp grasslands in western counties.

Population and conservation: The conservation of this scarce and localized colonial species is a major challenge. This is because of its specific requirement of abundant Devil's-bit Scabious in an extensive area of habitat subject to low intensity grazing. Its colonies are subject to huge fluctuations in size; a thriving colony with thousands of adults in one year may be extinct a few years later. Parasitic wasps are known to play a major role in such events.

Egg, caterpillar and chrysalis:

EGG (*page 209*): 0·7 mm (w) × 0·8 mm (h); pale yellow when fresh, darkening with age; laid in large batches on the undersides of the leaves of its foodplant.

CATERPILLAR (*page 216*): 26–30 mm; black, with reddish-brown legs; living communally in a silken web at first, solitary when fully-grown.

CHRYSALIS (*page 222*): 12–15 mm; greyish-white with yellow and black markings.

Foodplant: Devil's-bit Scabious.

Females are considerably larger than males and crawl, rather than fly, until they have laid their eggs.

A brightly coloured female showing the variation that ocurs in this species.

Best seen at known colonies on sunny days in mid-June, and easily approached when feeding.

Damp, tussocky grassland is favoured in western Britain.

UKBAP: PRIORITY
GB Red List: ENDANGERED
W&C Act: SALE PROHIBITED

Rare resident

Wingspan Male: 38–46 mm
              Female: 44–52 mm

♂♀

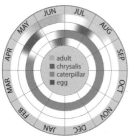

- adult
- chrysalis
- caterpillar
- egg

WHERE TO LOOK

The south coast of the Isle of Wight around Compton Bay near Freshwater and Wheeler's Bay near Ventnor. It is much more common on the continent, where it may be found in meadows and woodland margins.

LOOK-ALIKES

Marsh Fritillary (*page 110*)

This attractive butterfly is on the northernmost edge of its range in Britain and has always been our rarest fritillary.

Adult identification: The specialized habitat and restricted range of this species makes identification in the UK easy: it is confined to a few sites on undercliffs in the Isle of Wight, in south Hampshire and in the Channel Islands, where no other fritillaries are likely to be found. The butterfly can be identified by the delicate markings on the underside of its hindwing, which has a row of submarginal spots, a feature shared only with the Marsh Fritillary (*page 110*).

Behaviour: Males are among the most active and agile of butterflies, their flight being swift with glides interspersed by rapid wing-beats. Although the females tend to be less conspicuous, remaining hidden for long periods, they are also agile fliers.

Breeding habitat: On the Isle of Wight, this butterfly can be found in three distinct habitats. It is usually associated with warm, sheltered undercliffs, where land-slips have produced deep valleys, or chines, with a profusion of wildflowers, including its caterpillar foodplant and its favoured nectar plants, Common Bird's-foot-trefoil and Thrift. It can also be found on the tops of cliffs, and on south-facing downland, but undercliff colonies are larger and more permanent.

Population and conservation: Though vulnerable due to its restricted range, its status has changed little in recent decades. Since the early 1990s, a small colony has become established on the Hampshire coast. There have been many attempts to introduce this butterfly elsewhere, although all have been unsuccessful except for a small colony in Somerset. The species is largely dependent upon a transitory and unstable warm habitat, which allows the regular regrowth of fresh, young Ribwort Plantain plants favoured by the caterpillars.

Egg, caterpillar and chrysalis:

EGG (*page 209*): 0·4 mm (w) × 0·5 mm (h); thimble-shaped; yellow; laid in large batches on the underside of the leaves of its foodplant.

CATERPILLAR (*page 216*): 25 mm; black and bristly; gregarious, living in white silken webs.

CHRYSALIS (*page 222*): 13–15 mm; greyish-purple with black spots.

Foodplant: Ribwort Plantain.

Very active and easy to see in the right habitat, numbers peak in early June, but soon start to decline.

Although primarily restricted to the Isle of Wight, it is worth exploring suitable areas of the Hampshire coast.

Cliffs and undercliffs with Ribwort Plantain and plentiful nectar plants are preferred.

Small Pearl-bordered Fritillary

Boloria selene

| UKBAP: Priority |
| GB Red List: Near Threatened |
| **Declining resident** |

Wingspan Male: 35–41 mm
Female: 38–44 mm

♂♀

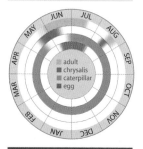

adult
chrysalis
caterpillar
egg

WHERE TO LOOK

In damp, sheltered areas in northern and western Britain where violets grow. Peak abundance is in mid-June, though usually later in Scotland.

LOOK-ALIKES

Pearl-bordered Fritillary
(*page 116*)
Glanville Fritillary (*page 112*)
Heath Fritillary (*page 108*)
Marsh Fritillary (*page 110*)
Wall (*page 142*)

Once a common butterfly throughout most of Britain, but now lost from much of its former range in the east. It remains widespread in Scotland and Wales.

Adult identification: This species is easily confused with the very similar Pearl-bordered Fritillary (*page 116*). Although there are some differences in the markings on the upperside of the wings, the most reliable field mark is the pattern of the hindwing underside. Small Pearl-bordered differs from Pearl-bordered in that the seven 'pearls' are edged with black chevrons (not red), and the centre of the hindwing, has an additional row of 'pearls' (not just two) which together create a more contrasting pattern. The populations in Scotland (race *insularum*) are brighter in appearance.

Behaviour: Males patrol with the typical gliding flight of the small fritillaries, keeping low and often pausing to sunbathe with wings spread wide. Egg-laying females flutter close to the ground, frequently alighting as they search for violets on which to lay their eggs.

Breeding habitat: In the south this species is usually found in woodland glades and clearings, while in the north and west damp grassland and moorland are favoured. Scottish colonies are usually found in sheep-grazed or deer-grazed open wood-pasture, usually with patches of Bracken and scrub. It also occurs in dune slacks and coastal cliffs. One of the violet species must always be present.

Population and conservation: Though widespread and locally abundant in Scotland, Wales and the West Country, numbers have declined dramatically elsewhere in southern England. The decline is thought to be due to the cessation of coppicing. In other parts of its range, the greatest threats are the loss of unfertilized damp grassland, and the degradation of moorland due to forestry and overgrazing.

Egg, caterpillar and chrysalis:
Egg (*page 209*): 0·5 mm (w) × 0·65 mm (h); conical and strongly ribbed; pale yellow; laid on or near violets.
Caterpillar (*page 216*): 21 mm; black, turning dark brown, with discontinuous white stripes and with yellowish spikes and black bristles.
Chrysalis (*page 222*): 15 mm; dark brown with silvery points.

Foodplants: usually Common Dog-violet or Marsh Violet.

The dark markings near the edge of the forewing are usually joined in Small Pearl-bordered Fritillary and separated in Pearl-bordered.

Small P-b Frit.

Pearl-b Frit.

M

F

Bugle is a favourite nectar source.

Grazed open wood-pasture with Bracken and scrub are the preferred habitat for the widespread, though threatened, Scottish race.

M *insularum*

M

F

The peak time to find patrolling males varies from late May in the south-west to early July in northern Scotland.

Heathland where Common Dog-violet can be found is a prime habitat in the west of Britain.

UKBAP: PRIORITY
GB Red List: ENDANGERED
W&C Act: SALE PROHIBITED

Threatened resident

Wingspan   Male: 38–46 mm
            Female: 43–47 mm

♂♀

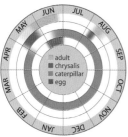

WHERE TO LOOK

Dartmoor in Devon remains a stronghold, another good site is Allt Mhuic in Inverness-shire. In Ireland it can be found in The Burren region, County Clare.

LOOK-ALIKES

Small Pearl-bordered Fritillary
    (page 114)
Glanville Fritillary (page 112)
Heath Fritillary (page 108)
Marsh Fritillary (page 110)
Wall (page 142)

The earliest of the British fritillaries to appear on the wing, usually emerging in early May in the south.

Adult identification: This species and the very similar Small Pearl-bordered Fritillary (*page 114*) are named after seven silver 'pearls' on the outer edge of the underside of the hindwings. Pearl-bordered differs from Small Pearl-bordered in that its seven 'pearls' are edged with red chevrons, not black. Also, in the centre of the hindwing there are only two additional 'pearls' instead of a band of seven. The largest 'pearl', together with a reddish area containing a small black spot, is said to resemble a duck's head. From above, the patterning at edge of the wing has a more 'open' appearance than that of the Small Pearl-bordered.

Behaviour: While females are generally inconspicuous, on warm days the males spend much of their time patrolling their territory, moving apparently effortlessly with glides and small, quick flaps of their wings. Both sexes are attracted to yellow and purple plants for nectaring, Bugle being particularly popular.

Breeding habitat: Three habitat types are favoured. All must have young violet plants growing on warm soil, usually under a bed of dead leaf-litter. In southern England, coppiced woodland clearings are used; in the West Country, well-drained grassland with Bracken and scrub; in Scotland, south-facing woodland edges with dense Bracken, and usually grazed by sheep or deer.

Population and conservation: One of our most rapidly declining butterflies. The virtual cessation of coppicing has been its downfall in southern and eastern England, but it often responds well when efforts are made to manage woodland for it. In the West Country, it depends on traditional low-intensity grazing, while in Scotland, efforts to increase the area of native woodland and the exclusion of sheep and deer may hasten its decline.

Egg, caterpillar and chrysalis:

EGG (*page 209*): 0·6 mm (w) × 0·8 mm (h); strongly ribbed; white or pale yellow; laid on or near violets.
CATERPILLAR (*page 216*): 20–25 mm; black, with a row of white spots on either side and black or yellow spines.
CHRYSALIS (*page 222*): 14 mm; like a dead leaf – grey-brown with silver spots.

Foodplant: usually Common Dog-violet.

In the south, emergence is usually in early May, sometimes April, but several weeks later in Scotland.

The two 'pearls' and characteristic 'duck's head' on the underside of the hindwing. ▶

A Pearl-bordered Fritillary in typical habitat.

UKBAP: Priority
GB Red List: Critically Endangered
W&C Act: Full Protection
Endangered resident
Wingspan: 55–65 mm

- adult
- chrysalis
- caterpillar
- egg

WHERE TO LOOK

Colonies are found on Dartmoor, Exmoor and the Malvern Hills but the easiest place to see this species is in the Lake District. Good sites include Arnside Knott and Whitbarrow in Cumbria, and Heddon's Mouth in Devon.

LOOK-ALIKES

Dark Freen Fritillary (*page 120*)
Silver-washed Fritillary (*page 122*)

One of our most endangered and rapidly declining butterflies, restricted almost entirely to western Britain, from the Lake District south to Dartmoor. There are thought to be fewer than 50 colonies remaining.

Adult identification: A large, bright fritillary, which can be confused with the Dark Green Fritillary (*page 120*). Separating the two is difficult unless you see the underside. The High Brown Fritillary takes its name from the brownish crescents around the outer silver patches on the underside of the hindwing, although the best field mark is the adjacent red-ringed silver spots, both features that the Dark Green Fritillary lacks. Females are slightly larger than males, and are less bright and more heavily marked with black.

Behaviour: Only really active in hot sunshine. Males have a fast, powerful flight, from which they divert to investigate anything resembling a female. They are not unduly aggressive or territorial. They are best approached while feeding, when often oblivious. Both sexes frequently soar among tree tops, roosting there at night and remaining there all day if the weather is poor.

Breeding habitat: Once regarded as chiefly a woodland butterfly, this species is now associated with areas of open scrub and rough grassland at woodland edges in western Britain. In Devon and Cornwall, bracken-covered south-facing slopes with violets are a favoured habitat.

Population and conservation: Following its rapid decline in the second half of the 20th century, this butterfly is being assisted by careful habitat management. Most of the Lake District colonies are within managed nature reserves and showing signs of recovery.

Egg, caterpillar and chrysalis:

Egg (*page 209*): 0·6 mm (w) × 0·8 mm (h); cone-shaped; pinkish-brown when first laid near the ground on twigs, dead leaves or stones, turning slate-grey with age.

Caterpillar (*page 216*): 38 mm; resembling a dead Bracken frond; pale, greenish-brown, sometimes dark, reddish-brown with a distinctive white line bordered by series of triangular black markings along the back.

Chrysalis (*page 222*): 20 mm; variegated dark to mid-brown, resembling a dead leaf.

Foodplant: usually Common Dog-violet.

The dark, shiny sex brands on the male's forewings are more conspicuous than those of the Dark Green Fritillary …

H B Frit.   D G Frit.

Males

…and there are also subtle differences in the shape of the forewing outer edge.

	Male	Female
High Brown Fritillary	very slightly concave	almost straight
Dark Green Fritillary (p. 120)	almost straight	slightly convex

M

Best looked for in hot sunshine, when most active.

In High Brown Fritillary the third spot on the upper forewing is indented from the two above it; in Dark Green Fritillary this spot is in line…

Females

H B Frit.

D G Frit.

…although the red-ringed silver spots on the underside of High Brown is the best distinguishing feature.

F

Often favours bracken-covered south-facing slopes.

M

F

Dark Green Fritillary

Argynnis aglaja

UKBAP: Not listed
GB Red List: Least concern

Widespread resident

Wingspan: 58–68 mm

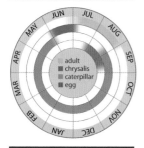

- adult
- chrysalis
- caterpillar
- egg

WHERE TO LOOK

Relatively easy to find in suitable habitat, especially the Scottish coastal dunes, the North and South Downs, and Exmoor and Dartmoor. Good sites include Heddon's Mouth in Devon, Martin Down in Hampshire and Horsey Dunes in Norfolk.

LOOK-ALIKES

High Brown Fritillary (*page 118*)
Silver-washed Fritillary (*page 122*)

A spectacular and widely distributed, fast-flying butterfly typical of downland and coastal dunes.

Adult identification: Very similar in size, shape and appearance to the High Brown Fritillary (*page 118*), and most readily separated by its much wider range. It favours open country and is a larger, more powerful butterfly than all our other fritillaries except the woodland-preferring Silver-washed Fritillary (*page 122*). The name derives from the distinctive green wash on the underwings, a feature common to both sexes. The golden ground colour of the upperwings tends to be paler in females, especially towards the edges. Females from Scotland, Ireland and the Isle of Man (race *scotica*) tend to be darker and more heavily marked.

Behaviour: An elegant, fast-flying butterfly. On warm, sunny days the males patrol their territory incessantly, their distinctive flight involving a number of rapid wing beats followed by a smooth, fast glide. The females tend to remain hidden in long grass until they are ready to lay their eggs, and have a more fluttering flight.

Breeding habitat: This is a butterfly of flower-rich unimproved grasslands with long vegetation, though it occasionally occurs in woodland rides and clearings. Its choice of habitat is surprisingly catholic, for it can be found on chalk and limestone downland, on acid grassland, moorland and (in Scotland particularly) on coastal dunes.

Population and conservation: Although this is the most widespread and common fritillary in Britain, its distribution has declined in central and eastern England since the 1970s, probably due to changing patterns of land use. However, its adaptability, and ability to tolerate wetter and cooler conditions than other fritillaries, has helped its survival. Loss of the flower-rich grasslands it favours, and the subsequent fragmentation of populations are its greatest threats.

Egg, caterpillar and chrysalis:

EGG (*page 209*): 0·8 mm (w) × 1·0 mm (h); cone-shaped; creamy yellow, becoming dull maroon; laid singly on or close to violets. CATERPILLAR (*page 216*): 35–40 mm; velvety black, with black spines and a row of orange-red spots along the flanks. CHRYSALIS (*page 222*): 20 mm; reddish-brown with black markings, and a distinctly curved abdomen.

Foodplant: Common Dog-violet, Hairy Violet or Marsh Violet.

Only really active on sunny days, when males are usually seen in flight.

The best time to see Dark Green Fritillaries nectaring is early or late in the day, when they are attracted to purple flowers.

They will sometimes remain on the same flower for several minutes at a time.

The male sex brands are less conspicuous than those of the High Brown Fritillary …

M

Primarily a butterfly of flower-rich grasslands; males tend to be a richer colour than females.

…and there are also subtle differences in the shape of the forewing outer edge in both sexes (see *page 119*).

F

Females are generally out-of-sight, hidden in long grass.

F

The green wash to the underside is the most apparent feature that distinguishes this species from the similar High Brown Fritillary (*page 118*).

M

M

Silver-washed Fritillary

Argynnis paphia

UKBAP: Not listed
GB Red List: Least concern
Localized resident

Wingspan Male: 69–76 mm
Female: 73–80 mm

♂♀

This handsome butterfly is the largest of the British fritillaries. Its range is increasing once again after a long period of decline in the 20th century.

Adult identification: The easiest of our fritillaries to identify, due to its large size, distinctive flight and preferred habitat. The rich golden-brown wings with clear black markings are typical of a fritillary, but the subtle silver washes on the underwing of both sexes separate it from other species. Males have four black ridges of scent scales on the veins of each forewing. Females have more extensive, heavier black markings, and look rather darker than the male. A distinctive form of the female called *valezina* (see *page 37*) occurs in some populations, particularly in central-southern England.

Behaviour: A powerful butterfly with a fast, gliding flight. Adults often fly high around the tops of trees, but they will readily drop down in search of nectar (Bramble is particularly popular), or to chase a potential mate. When feeding they can be approached readily. Though most active when the sun is shining, they will still fly on lightly overcast days. Females venture into shadier parts of the woodland to lay their eggs.

Breeding habitat: This is a butterfly of broad-leaved woodland, particularly favouring sunny rides and glades in oak woods. However, in Somerset, Devon, Cornwall and southern Ireland, it is not unusual to find this species wandering along well-wooded hedgerows and sheltered, sunken lanes.

WHERE TO LOOK

It is worth checking any large oak woodland in southern or western England and in Ireland. The New Forest is a good area, but this species is not as abundant there as it once was.

LOOK-ALIKES

Dark Green Fritillary (*page 120*)
High Brown Fritillary (*page 118*)

Population and conservation: Much more common in Victorian times than it is today, its range even extending as far north as Scotland. This contracted markedly between then and the 1970s, and while the range has expanded since, its population has not increased significantly.

Egg, caterpillar and chrysalis:
Egg (*page 209*): 1·0 mm (w) × 1·0 mm (h); laid singly in the crevices of the bark of tree trunks.
Caterpillar (*page 216*): 38 mm; dark brown with two yellow stripes and with reddish-brown spines.
Chrysalis (*page 222*): 22 mm; as with other fritillaries, camouflaged to resemble a dead leaf and extremely difficult to find.

Foodplants: violets, especially Common Dog-violet.

M

Females lack the dark lines of the male's forewing.

F

Ad

The largest of our fritillaries, which will readily descend from the tree tops to nectar on Bramble.

Although primarily found in oakwoods, it can often be seen along tall hedgerows and sunken lanes in south-west England and Ireland.

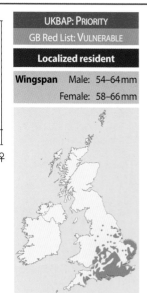

UKBAP: PRIORITY
GB Red List: VULNERABLE

Localized resident

Wingspan Male: 54–64 mm
Female: 58–66 mm

♂♀

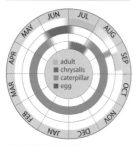

- adult
- chrysalis
- caterpillar
- egg

WHERE TO LOOK

Woodlands in Hants, Dorset, Sussex and Surrey, but also in the Midlands and East Anglia. Reliable sites here include Monkwood in Worcs., Holt Country Park in Norfolk, Chambers Farm Wood in Lincs., and Fermyn Woods in Northants.

LOOK-ALIKES

Purple Emperor (*page 126*)

An elegant and distinctive inhabitant of sunny woodland glades, particularly in southern England. Although its range has spread, the overall population appears to be declining.

Adult identification: Easy to identify when close, but from a distance it can be mistaken for a Purple Emperor (*page 126*). Although their uppersides are similar, the hindwings lack the 'eye' of the larger Purple Emperor. The wings are also more rounded than Purple Emperor and it has a daintier, gliding flight. The sexes are almost identical. Some rare aberrations occur (see *page 37*).

Behaviour: Unrivalled among British butterflies for their graceful and agile flight, adults propelling themselves with a quick whirr of the wings, followed by long glides. Though they spend a lot of time in the tree canopy, they occasionally come down to ground level, where they are particularly attracted by Bramble blossom.

Breeding habitat: This butterfly favours sunny rides in broad-leaved woodland in the southern half of England. However, it can also be found in young coniferous plantations, before the growing trees shade out the ground cover. Its key requirement is a plentiful supply of Honeysuckle, the caterpillar's foodplant, although this butterfly is often strangely absent from woods where conditions appear ideal.

Population and conservation: This is a species that has extended its range northwards over the last 50 years or so, and is now found in Suffolk, Norfolk, Lincolnshire and the West Midlands. However, population counts at monitored sites have shown a decrease in more recent years and there is concern about its future. There is also a potentially serious threat from the loss of its foodplant to browsing deer. Because population densities are usually low, it is unusual to see more than two or three individuals at a time.

Egg, caterpillar and chrysalis:

EGG (*page 210*): 0·9 mm (w) × 0·9 mm (h); spherical; olive-green; laid singly.

CATERPILLAR (*page 216*): 25–29 mm; spiny; brown, turning bright green after the final moult, with a whitish line along each side.

CHRYSALIS (*page 223*): 22 mm; unusually shaped, and coloured green and brown, resembling a dead Honeysuckle leaf.

Foodplant: Honeysuckle.

F

M

Peak abundance is in July.

Best looked for in sunny rides or glades in deciduous woodlands with a dominance of oaks and Hazel, and where Honeysuckle grows.

Most frequently seen well when feeding on patches of Bramble.

M

F

| UKBAP: Not listed |
| GB Red List: NEAR THREATENED |
| W&C Act: SALE PROHIBITED |

Localized resident

Wingspan Male: 70–78 mm
Female: 76–92 mm

♂♀

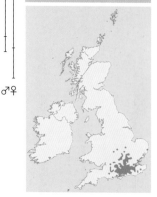

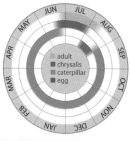

adult
chrysalis
caterpillar
egg

WHERE TO LOOK

Mature woodlands in the Surrey and Sussex Weald, and in larger woods in central southern England. Classic sites are Bentley Wood in Wiltshire, Alice Holt Forest in Surrey and Fermyn Woods in Northamptonshire.

LOOK-ALIKES

White Admiral (*page 124*)

A beautiful and iconic woodland butterfly, which although scarce and localized appears to be expanding its range.

Adult identification: With a good view, there is no mistaking a male Purple Emperor, due to a combination of its large size, distinctive white-on-black markings, and glorious purple sheen, although this can only be seen at certain angles as it depends on the refraction of light by its wing scales. The female is slightly larger, has bolder markings, and lacks the purple sheen. Colour variations are rare.

Behaviour: Males will remain around a so-called 'master tree', usually an oak, which may be used every year. Here, they perch, wings half-open, waiting to intercept a passing female, or chase off a rival male. Both sexes normally feed on aphid honeydew and tree sap. Males are best observed in the morning, usually between about 10 and 11 am, particularly at the beginning of the flight season. At this time, they sometimes descend to the ground to probe the surface with their tongues, apparently to absorb salts; they are also attracted to rotting flesh and animal excrement.

Breeding habitat: Seldom found far from mature deciduous or mixed forest, though wandering individuals may occasionally be encountered following hedgerows, or even crossing open fields. The key requirement is a plentiful supply of their caterpillars' foodplants.

Population and conservation: For much of the 20th century, this species declined throughout its range in southern England. In recent years there has been a welcome resurgence, and a modest re-expansion. Its survival depends on the sensitive management of ancient woodland, and the retention of willows.

Egg, caterpillar and chrysalis:
EGG (*page 210*): 1·2 mm (w) × 1·0 mm (h); dome-shaped; green; laid singly on the foodplant.
CATERPILLAR (*page 217*): 35–40 mm; very well camouflaged: green when first hatched but by November has turned brown ready for winter hibernation. In the spring, post-hibernation caterpillars gradually become green again. They have distinctive 'horns' on their heads.
CHRYSALIS (*page 223*): 30–35 mm; pale green, closely resembling a willow leaf.

Foodplants: usually Goat Willow, sometimes Common Willow.

A mature woodland specialist.

Often comes to ground late morning.

Red Admiral

Vanessa atalanta

UKBAP: Not listed
GB Red List: Least concern
Abundant migrant

Wingspan Male: 64–72 mm
Female: 70–78 mm

♂♀

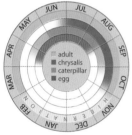

WHERE TO LOOK

Almost anywhere, often in numbers on flowering buddleias in late summer and fallen fruit in the autumn. Individuals can become 'drunk' when feeding on fermenting fruit and be finger-tame.

LOOK-ALIKES

At a distance:
Peacock (*page 134*)
Painted Lady (*page 130*)
Small Tortoiseshell (*page 132*)

This stunning butterfly is a familiar and widespread species, although numbers each year depend on migration from continental Europe.

Adult identification: Unmistakable, for no other British butterfly has the same distinctive combination of black, white and red. The sexes are similar although males are slightly smaller.

Behaviour: A strongly migratory species: the British population depends almost entirely on immigration each year from continental Europe, for very few adults manage to hibernate successfully here. The first major influxes are in late May and early June. Females arrive already mated, and it is their offspring that we see in the summer and autumn. This species is usually at its most abundant in September, when fallen fruit will often attract considerable numbers. In mild, sunny autumns, it is not unusual to see Red Admirals on the wing well into November. Many undertake a southerly migration back towards the continent at this time.

Breeding habitat: An adaptable species that can occur in almost any flower-rich habitat throughout Britain. Gardens with flowering buddleias and fruit trees are particularly popular. It prefers vigorous young Common Nettles for breeding.

Population and conservation: In most years this is one of our commonest and most widespread butterflies. Numbers have increased in recent years and given the abundance of its foodplants, the future of this magnificent butterfly seems assured.

Egg, caterpillar and chrysalis:
EGG (*page 210*): 0·6 mm (w) × 0·8 mm (h); light-green, turning grey; laid singly on the upper surfaces of the leaves of its foodplant.

CATERPILLAR (*page 217*): 35 mm; solitary, and occurs in several colour forms, ranging from black through brown to grey with yellow; its branched spines are mainly of a pale tint.

CHRYSALIS (*page 223*): 22–24 mm; invariably found at the top of a nettle, within a feeding shelter made by the caterpillar. This is the easiest chrysalis to find of any British butterfly.

Foodplant: Common Nettle.

There may be a small white spot in the scarlet band of the forewing of some individuals, usually females.

Though a few overwinter successfully, this butterfly is essentially a migrant from continental Europe.

Most abundant in late summer and frequently seen feeding on fallen fruit well into the autumn if the weather remains mild.

Painted Lady

Vanessa cardui

UKBAP: Not listed	
GB Red List: Least concern	

Regular migrant

Wingspan Male: 58–70 mm
Female: 62–74 mm

♂♀

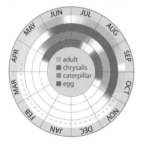

- adult
- chrysalis
- caterpillar
- egg

WHERE TO LOOK

Due to its strong migratory instincts, this butterfly may be found virtually anywhere. Individuals are often attracted to flowering buddleias and other garden flowers in late summer, when they can allow a close approach.

LOOK-ALIKES

At a distance:
Small Tortoiseshell (*page 132*)
Large fritillaries
(*pages 118–123*)

A handsome migrant butterfly that in some years is common throughout much of Britain and Ireland, but in others is scarce or even absent.

Adult identification: An easy butterfly to identify, thanks to a combination of its powerful flight and distinctive colouring. However, it should be noted that adults vary significantly in size and that the beautiful salmon-pink of a freshly emerged individual fades to orange-brown during its long life. Badly faded and tatty individuals are not uncommon.

Behaviour: A highly migratory species, with the first butterflies of the year to reach us probably direct migrants from North Africa. It has a fast and powerful flight and is able to travel considerable distances. Once settled, males establish themselves in a territory, vigorously investigating any object that attracts their attention. Both sexes feed frequently on flowers, and in years of abundance it is not uncommon to see many individuals feeding together.

Breeding habitat: This wide-ranging migrant can occur anywhere, but it favours dry, open areas, particularly rough ground with thistles, and usually avoids woodlands.

Population and conservation: The British and Irish population depends wholly upon migration. In an exceptional year, millions may occur, even extending as far north as Orkney and Shetland. It is thought that a proportion of butterflies attempt the reverse migration in the autumn. Although an adult has been recorded overwintering in Cornwall, the British and Irish population effectively dies out each winter; recolonization depends on immigration the following spring.

Egg, caterpillar and chrysalis:

EGG (*page 210*): 0·6 mm (w) × 0·65 mm (h); oval; light-green, turning grey and relatively easy to find on its foodplants.
CATERPILLAR (*page 217*): 30 mm; solitary; black with yellow spines and a thin yellow line along each side. It spins a succession of silk tents under leaves, before finally emerging to feed openly after its last moult.
CHRYSALIS (*page 223*): 25 mm; usually brownish-grey and suspended under a leaf.

Foodplants: thistles.

A long-lived butterfly; fresh individuals are salmon-pink, fading to pale orange with age.

The strong-flying Painted Lady is a migrant from North Africa and can be seen the length and breadth of Britain and Ireland.

The numbers arriving each year are dependent upon many factors, and while some years there may be thousands, in others there may be just a few.

The first arrivals breed and give rise to a late summer generation, but this is unable to survive the winter so the British population each year is dependent on immigration.

Small Tortoiseshell

Aglais urticae

| UKBAP: Not listed |
| GB Red List: Least concern |

Abundant resident

Wingspan Male: 42–48 mm
Female: 46–52 mm

♂♀

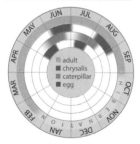

- adult
- chrysalis
- caterpillar
- egg

WHERE TO LOOK

Look first in gardens, where flowering buddleias and other flowers often prove to be an irresistible draw. Often found hibernating in dark, dry corners, where they should be left undisturbed.

LOOK-ALIKES

Large Tortoiseshell (*page 184*)
Painted Lady (*page 130*)
Red Admiral (*page 128*)
Comma (*page 136*)

This attractive and familiar butterfly is widely distributed throughout Britain and Ireland and can be found in almost every month of the year.

Adult identification: Readily identified by its striking and attractive pattern, shared by both sexes. Look for the delightful blue edges to both wings. Given close views, this species can only really be confused with the exceedingly rare migrant Large Tortoiseshell (*page 184*), which is larger, duller, and lacks the white spots on the forewing. Some rare aberrations occur (see *page 36*).

Behaviour: This species hibernates as an adult, and usually emerges for the first time on warm, sunny days in March or April, though earlier sightings are not uncommon in southern England. Males tend to be more mobile in the morning, when they feed and bask in the sun. In the afternoon they set up temporary territories, which they defend against rivals, and court passing females. In contrast, individuals that are going to hibernate show no interest in courtship, but spend their days feeding up in preparation for hibernation, which they will enter as early as late July or August.

Breeding habitat: A cosmopolitan butterfly, which can be found almost anywhere, from the tops of mountains to city centres.

Population and conservation: Though this butterfly seems always to have been widespread, numbers do fluctuate markedly from year to year, sometimes due to the depredations of parasitic wasps. Southern populations have at least two and sometimes three broods a year; given the abundance of its foodplants, its future in Britain and Ireland looks secure.

Egg, caterpillar and chrysalis:

Egg (*pages 210, 211*): 0·75 (w) × 0·85 mm (h); green; laid in large clusters on the underside of leaves of its foodplant. They match the leaf colour closely, but turn yellow before the caterpillars hatch 1–3 weeks later, depending on ambient temperature.

Caterpillar (*page 217*): 32 mm; black, finely dotted with white, and with broken bands of yellow. These are warning colours, for the body contains poisons. The caterpillars are found in groups in white silken webs, which are easy to spot in patches of nettles.

Chrysalis (*page 223*): 20–22 mm; variable in colour from grey to brown.

Foodplants: Common Nettle, Small Nettle and sometimes Hop.

The sexes are identical in appearance, though females are larger than males.

Small Tortoiseshells feeding in late summer in preparation for hibernation is a familar sight throughout Britain and Ireland.

UKBAP: Not listed
GB Red List: Least concern

Abundant resident

Wingspan Male: 63–68 mm
Female: 67–75 mm

♂♀

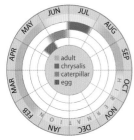

adult
chrysalis
caterpillar
egg

WHERE TO LOOK

May be found almost anywhere, but sheltered woodland clearings and gardens are favoured. It can be attracted in numbers to flowering buddleias.

LOOK-ALIKES

At a distance:
Red Admiral (*page 128*)
Comma (*page 136*)
Painted Lady (*page 130*)

A handsome and familiar butterfly found throughout Britain and Ireland, which is continuing to expand its range northwards.

Adult identification: Unmistakable thanks to the large 'eyes' in the corner of both front and hindwings. Unless the sun is shining directly on it, the beautifully camouflaged underside appears almost black.

Behaviour: This species hibernates as an adult and is one of the first butterflies on the wing on warm spring days. After feeding during the morning, males establish territories, from which they see off intruding males or pursue females. For summer adults, the chief preoccupation is feeding in preparation for hibernation, which they usually enter in early September. Dark, sheltered crevices in trees, garden sheds or even church towers are sought out for hibernation. Adults flash their wings at potential enemies, using its 'eyes' to warn them off. It can also rub its forewings and hindwings together to generate a warning sound.

Breeding habitat: Almost anywhere, for this is a highly adaptable species. The best sites are where favoured nectar plants are plentiful – willows in spring, and teasels, thistles and buddleias in summer. Large nettle patches are required for egg-laying.

Population and conservation: This widespread species is continuing to extend its range northwards and appears to be thriving in Britain and Ireland, although populations do dip in some years.

Egg, caterpillar and chrysalis:

Egg (*page 210*): 0·7 mm (w) × 0·8 mm (h); laid in large batches on the underside of nettle leaves.

Caterpillar (*page 217*): 42 mm; black with white-speckles and long black spines; found in groups within a silken web until fully-grown, when they may be found singly.

Chrysalis (*page 223*): 25–29 mm; variable in colour, from pale green to brownish-grey, stippled with black. It is difficult to find in the wild because the caterpillar usually wanders some distance (several metres) from its foodplant before pupating.

Foodplant: Common Nettle.

The ubiquitous Peacock is attracted to a host of garden flowers.

Common resident

Wingspan:	50–64 mm

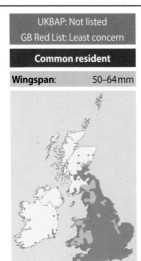

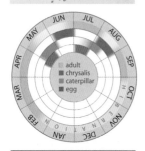

- adult
- chrysalis
- caterpillar
- egg

WHERE TO LOOK

Anywhere in suitable habitat, particularly in the southern half of Britain. It is attracted to willow catkins in spring, flowering buddleias in summer, and fallen fruit in autumn.

LOOK-ALIKES

Fritillaries (*pages 108–123*)
Wall (*page 142*)
Small Tortoiseshell (*page 132*)
Painted Lady (*page 130*)
Red Admiral (*page 128*)
Peacock (*page 134*)

A century ago, this handsome butterfly was a rarity in Britain, but since then it has enjoyed a reversal in its fortunes and is now common throughout the country.

Adult identification: With its wings closed, this is a well camouflaged butterfly, resembling a dead, ragged leaf. There is a distinctive white 'comma' mark on the underwing that gives this species its name. The adults come in two colour forms: early spring caterpillars produce the form *hutchinsoni*, which have golden-brown undersides, whereas the later-emerging adults are rich tawny-red. Their gliding flight and colouration can suggest a fritillary, but the scalloped wing shape is unmistakable.

Behaviour: Hibernating as an adult, this is one of the first butterflies to be seen on the wing, often emerging in late February or early March. Early-emerging individuals of the spring generation breed and produce a second generation, while later-emerging individuals and all the second generation overwinter. Males feed early in the morning and again in the late afternoon, but spend much of the day patrolling in search of a mate. Their flight is fast, with a rapid whirr of wings, followed by long glides.

Breeding habitat: This species likes open woodland and woodland edges, but is often found in gardens.

Population and conservation: The fall and rise of this species' population still intrigues entomologists, and has never been satisfactorily explained. There has been a significant increase in numbers in recent years, and it is one of the few British butterflies to have expanded its range. However, it is still only occasionally found in Ireland.

Egg, caterpillar and chrysalis:

EGG (*page 210*): 0·65 mm (w) × 0·8 mm (h); laid singly on the upperside of a leaf of its foodplant.
CATERPILLAR (*page 217*): 32–35 mm; black, banded with orange-brown and with a distinctive white splash on the back making it resemble a bird dropping. At first it feeds on the underside of a leaf, but when larger it feeds exclusively on the upper surface.
CHRYSALIS (*page 223*): 21 mm; resembles the underwing of the adult, with a beautiful dead-leaf camouflage.

Foodplants: Common Nettle, Hop, elms, currants, willows.

M

F

▲ *Spring form f.* hutchinsoni

Summer form ▼

M

F

Can be found readily from February until hibernation at the end of September.

Ad

Ad f. *hutchinsoni*

Marbled White

Melanargia galathea

| UKBAP: Not listed |
| GB Red List: Least concern |

Widesrpead resident

| Wingspan | Male: | 53 mm |
| | Female: | 58 mm |

♂♀

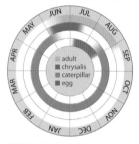

| adult |
| chrysalis |
| caterpillar |
| egg |

WHERE TO LOOK

Most common in Dorset, Wiltshire, Somerset and Devon, and found wherever there is suitable habitat. Elsewhere, its range is more localized. The best time to look is in mid-July, when numbers peak.

LOOK-ALIKES

Whites (*pages 62–71*)

This attractive and distinctive butterfly is widespread in southern England and parts of southern Wales, and has been extending its range both northwards and eastwards in recent years.

Adult identification: Though there are several very similar species to be found in southern Europe, in Britain there is no other species that can be confused with this black-and-white butterfly.

Behaviour: A colonial species, sometimes found in large numbers. In the early morning and late afternoon, both sexes will sunbathe, perched on grass-heads or prominent flowers. When sunbathing, they are highly approachable, taking little or no notice of observers. In the heat of the day and in bright sunshine adults feed with their wings closed tightly. This butterfly has a distinctive slow, flapping flight.

Breeding habitat: Typically, unimproved grassland, usually on chalk or limestone. They often occur on coastal grasslands, and may also be found on roadside verges or railway embankments.

Population and conservation: This ia a butterfly that has been increasing and extending its range, although there have been some losses. Nevertheless, its distribution in Britain remains patchy and it is absent from large areas of eastern and northern England, most of Scotland, and Ireland. This is puzzling because the species has shown an ability to make use of new habitats where there is flowery grassland, including waste ground and uncultivated field margins.

Egg, caterpillar and chrysalis:
EGG (*page 211*): 1·0 mm (w) × 1·0 mm (w); spherical; pale green to white; scattered near to the foodplants.
CATERPILLAR (*page 218*): 28 mm; pale brown or yellowish-green, with two darkish lines along the back and a lighter-coloured line along each side.
CHRYSALIS (*page 224*): 12–15 mm; pale brown, formed on the surface of the ground, or sometimes under moss.

Foodplants: usually Red Fescue, also Sheep's-fescue, Yorkshire-fog and Tor-grass.

M

M

Females are larger than males.

F

F

Conspicuous when basking on sunny July and August days in early morning or late afternoon.

Typical Marbled White habitat.

Speckled Wood

Pararge aegeria

UKBAP: Not listed
GB Red List: Least concern

Common resident

Wingspan	Male: 46–52 mm
	Female: 48–56 mm

♂♀

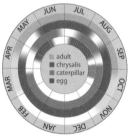

- adult
- chrysalis
- caterpillar
- egg

WHERE TO LOOK

In any suitable habitat within its range. Look along woodland edges and hedges where there are patches of sunshine and shade. It is most abundant in late August.

LOOK-ALIKES

Wall (*page 142*)
Grayling (*page 144*)

An attractive woodland butterfly that flies in dappled shade. After range contractions during the late 19th and early 20th century, it has been steadily regaining ground.

Adult identification: The cream-on-chocolate wings make this an easy butterfly to identify. Females are larger than males and have larger cream patches. The depth of their chocolate colour is variable in both sexes, some butterflies being darker than others. The first butterflies to emerge each year tend to be paler than those that emerge later. Uppersides of the larger Scottish race (*oblita*) are darker with paler patches; those from the Isles of Scilly (race *insula*) have larger, more orange-coloured patches.

Behaviour: This species' habit of drinking honeydew high in the tree canopy goes largely unobserved, but in spring and late summer (when honeydew is in short supply), individuals will take nectar from flowers. Males spend their days either basking in patches of sunlight near or on the ground, or patrolling their breeding territory. In woodlands where sunlit patches are at a premium, males defend these vigorously. This is the only British butterfly to hibernate both as a caterpillar and as a chrysalis. The emergence of first and second-generation butterflies therefore overlaps.

Breeding habitat: Typically a common butterfly of woodland rides and glades, but can also be found along hedgerows and even in gardens.

Population and conservation: This species is found throughout Britain and Ireland. Its range has been spreading since the 1920s, particularly to the north and east and in Scotland. Numbers tend to increase following wet summers, but fall after drought years.

Egg, caterpillar and chrysalis:
Egg (*page 211*): 0·8 mm (w) × 0·8 mm (h); almost spherical, pale, and laid singly. In spring and early autumn, eggs are laid on plants in open, sunlit situations; in summer they are laid on plants in shaded woodland.
Caterpillar (*page 218*): 28 mm; yellowish-green, with a central dark green stripe along the back and thin yellow lines along each side.
Chrysalis (*page 224*): 18 mm; A delicate shade of green.

Foodplants: a variety of grasses, though Cock's-foot, Yorkshire-fog and False Brome are preferred.

▲ 1st generation   2nd ▼

M

F

M

F

M *oblita*

M *insula*

M

F

Wall

Lasiommata megera

UKBAP: PRIORITY
GB Red List: NEAR THREATENED

Localized resident

Wingspan: 45–53 mm

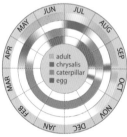

Though widely distributed, this butterfly tends to be both localized and scarce. Since the 1970s, it has been lost from many inland areas in both central and southern England, but has maintained its numbers on and around the coast and even expanded in more northerly areas.

Adult identification: With its fast, flashing flight and golden forewings this species suggests a fritillary (*pages 108–123*) or Comma (*page 136*). However, when seen at rest its bright 'eye' spots confirm its identity as one of the 'browns'. The females are slightly larger and paler than males but lack the dark band of scent scales that males have on the upperside of their forewings. This is by far the most showy and active of all the British brown butterflies.

Behaviour: The male spends much of his life patrolling in search of virgin females, pausing to feed on whatever flowers he passes. The gliding flight is fast and low. On cooler days, males spend much of their time basking in sunny, sheltered spots, such as south-facing walls (hence the name). The females are considerably less active.

Breeding habitat: A species that favours short, open grassland, where it is usually found on stony tracks, or where the turf is broken. It also likes coastal habitats, such as cliffs, as well as disturbed land, ranging from quarries to gardens.

Population and conservation: The loss of unimproved grassland has led to a marked decline in numbers inland, but the cause of its recent disappearance in parts of the south is not well understood. Its coastal populations seem to be doing well. This is a species that thrives in hot summers, and suffers in cool and damp conditions. There is evidence that it is expanding its range northwards.

WHERE TO LOOK

Most easily located around the coasts of England and Wales, where it tends to be most abundant. Suitably sunny inland sites such as railway embankments are also worth checking.

LOOK-ALIKES

Fritillaries (*pages 108–123*)
Comma (*page 136*)
Speckled Wood (*page 140*)
Grayling (*page 144*)

Egg, caterpillar and chrysalis:
EGG (*page 211*): 0·9 mm (w) × 0·9 mm (h); almost spherical; greenish-white, and laid singly or in clusters.
CATERPILLAR (*page 218*): 24 mm; bright green, with thin whitish-yellow stripes.
CHRYSALIS (*page 224*): 16 mm; variable in colour from green to blackish; attached to plant stems.

Foodplants: a variety of grasses including bents, Yorkshire-fog and Cock's-foot.

Highly active when warm; on cooler days look for basking butterflies in sheltered south-facing spots.

More easily found in areas of short open grassland near the coast.

× 1½ **Grayling**   *Hipparchia semele*

| UKBAP: Priority |
| GB Red List: Vulnerable |

| **Declining resident** |

Wingspan   Male: 51–56 mm
Female: 54–62 mm

♂♀

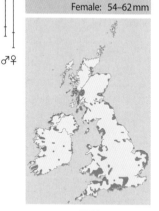

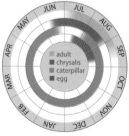

- adult
- chrysalis
- caterpillar
- egg

WHERE TO LOOK

Most easily located at coastal sites, particularly in southern and western Britain, or on heathland in southern England where it can be abundant. It also occurs locally around the coast of Britain and Ireland.

LOOK-ALIKES

Speckled Wood (*page 140*)
Wall (*page 142*)

This cryptic yet distinctive butterfly is widespread and reasonably common around the coast of Britain and Ireland, but has declined in many inland areas.

Adult identification: Almost invariably settles with the wings closed, so the broad yellow bands on the forewings of the female, or the dark sex brands on the forewings of the male may only be seen in flight. The underside of the hindwing is similar in both sexes, and provides perfect camouflage on bare ground. There are regional differences, with several races being recognised (see *page 229*). The most interesting is race *thyone*, which occurs only on the Great Orme in North Wales. This looks like other Graylings but is distinctly smaller and emerges several weeks earlier.

Behaviour: A fast-flying species with a distinctive gliding flight, often encountered when flushed from open ground. As soon as it lands it shuts its wings, the 'eye' spot on the underside of the forewing being visible briefly before being drawn down out of sight behind the hindwings. The female is secretive, so most sightings are of males. They are attracted to puddles, and when drinking, are easy to approach closely. In cool weather, this species spends a lot of time sunbathing, turning their bodies to catch the sun, while in hot sunshine they face the sun to minimize the sun's heat.

Breeding habitat: A colonial species usually found on coastal dunes or undercliffs. Inland colonies tend to be on dry heathland, chalk or limestone grassland, earthworks or in quarries. Its one essential requirement is dry, well-drained soil with lots of bare ground.

Population and conservation: While most coastal colonies continue to flourish, this species has suffered from loss of habitat at many of its inland sites. Improved management of heathland may well help it to survive. However, the species is in overall decline, and its future seems uncertain.

Egg, caterpillar and chrysalis:

Egg (*page 211*): 0·7 mm (w) × 0·8 mm (h); oval-shaped and strongly ribbed; pale; laid singly on foodplant or nearby debris.
Caterpillar (*page 218*): 30 mm; yellowish-white with light brown longitudinal stripes; feeds at night.
Chrysalis (*page 224*): 16 mm; reddish-brown; formed below ground in a hollow lined with silk.

Foodplants: wide variety of grasses in sunny, open positions.

144

Camouflaged males are usually encountered when flushed from a path; females are more secretive.

▲ Males in characteristic pose with the 'eye' spotted forewing barely visible.

▲ The slightly smaller Great Orme race thyone emerges at the end of June.

Well-drained grassland with lots of bare ground is the favoured habitat.

Gatekeeper

Pyronia tithonus

(Hedge Brown)

UKBAP: Not listed
GB Red List: Least concern

Common resident

Wingspan   Male: 37–43 mm
             Female: 42–48 mm

♂♀

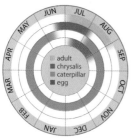

adult
chrysalis
caterpillar
egg

WHERE TO LOOK

Readily found anywhere in suitable habitat in the southern half of Britain. It is extending its range northwards.

LOOK-ALIKES

Meadow Brown (*page 148*)
Small Heath (*page 156*)
Large Heath (*page 158*)

A widespread and highly successful species throughout the southern half of Britain, and one that has been extending its range northwards in recent years.

Adult identification: Though often confused with the larger and duller Meadow Brown (*page 148*), this species is easy to identify thanks to its much brighter colouring, with distinctive orange-on-chocolate patterning on both the forewing and the hindwing. There are distinctive white dots on the underside of the hindwings (these are black on the Meadow Brown). The male is smaller than the female and displays a broad band of dark scales (the sex-brand) on the forewing.

Behaviour: A colonial species, often found in abundance, though some colonies may be very small. The flight period is quite precise, starting in mid-July, peaking in early August, and finishing by the end of that month. This is a sedentary butterfly, which is rarely found far from its colony. They frequently sunbathe with their wings open, a feature that distinguishes this species from the Meadow Brown.

Breeding habitat: The alternative name of Hedge Brown gives a good indication of the favoured habitat, for this species is always associated with shrubs. Colonies are usually found along hedgerows or in scrubby woodland with plenty of wide and sunny rides.

Population and conservation: Common and widespread, but vulnerable to agricultural intensification and hedgerow removal.

Egg, caterpillar and chrysalis:

EGG (*page 211*): 0·65 mm (w) × 0·7 mm (h); barrel-shaped; white, mottling with age until becoming brown, laid singly on grass blades or just dropped into long grass at the base of shrubs.

CATERPILLAR (*page 218*): 25 mm; variable in colour, starting grey, turning green and then either light grey-green or pale yellow-brown, and often speckled; covered with very fine hairs.

CHRYSALIS (*page 224*): 12 mm; cream with brown markings, but hidden under a leaf, so rarely found in the wild.

Foodplants: a range of grasses, mainly bents, fescues and meadow-grasses.

Look for colonies in areas with scrubby hedgerows and tall grasses from mid-July to August.

The double white specks in the 'eye' spots distinguish the Gatekeeper from other similar species.

Ragwort is a favoured
nectar source.

UKBAP: Not listed
GB Red List: Least concern

Abundant resident

Wingspan   Male: 40–55 mm
          Female: 42–60 mm

♂♀

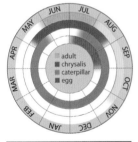

WHERE TO LOOK

Almost anywhere in
Britain and Ireland, except
Shetland.

LOOK-ALIKES

Gatekeeper (*page 146*)
Scotch Argus (*page 154*)
Ringlet (*page 150*)
Grayling (*page 144*)
Small Heath (*page 156*)

The familiar Meadow Brown is not only one of our most
widespread butterflies, but often the most abundant, too.
However, colonies are vulnerable to intensive farming,
and the loss of the unimproved grassland they favour.

Adult identification: The male is typically a dark, plain
butterfly, with all chocolate-brown wings relieved only by a tiny
'eye' spot in the corner of the forewing. The larger female has
a bright orange blaze on the forewing. Resting females often
perch with their wings closed and overlapping so that their 'eye'
spot is hidden. Old individuals are often heavily faded. There
are a number of races; butterflies from the Isle of Man and
north-west Scotland (*splendida*) are darker; those from Ireland
(*iernes*) and the Isles of Scilly (*cassiteridum*) are larger.

Behaviour: A slow-flying, meandering butterfly that seldom
rises more than a metre above the ground. It will fly on dull
days, even in light rain, when few other species are active.
A resting female often raises her forewings to reveal the bright
'eyes' as a defence against predators.

Breeding habitat: Typically a butterfly of open grasslands,
but this is a highly adaptable and successful species, well able
to adjust to a variety of different habitats where its foodplants
can be found. Such habitats include roadside verges, woodland
rides and parks, gardens and cemeteries in urban areas.

Population and conservation: A widespread and successful
species, and the one recorded as most abundant according
to results gathered by the Butterfly Monitoring Scheme.
Colonies are, however, vulnerable to agricultural intensification.

Egg, caterpillar and chrysalis:
Egg (*page 211*): 0·5 mm (w) × 0·5 mm (h); a slightly flattened,
ribbed sphere; brownish-yellow turning greyish in colour;
laid singly on the grass blades.
Caterpillar (*page 218*): 25 mm; pale green above, darker
below, with an off-white stripe along each side.
Chrysalis (*page 224*): 16 mm; variable, sometimes striped, but
often simply plain green.

Foodplants: a range of grasses including bents, fescues,
Meadow-grasses, Cock's-foot and False Brome.

The Meadow Brown is Britain's most abundant butterfly and can be found almost anywhere.

Meadow Brown has single white speck in the underwing 'eye' spot and black specks on the hindwing.

The Meadow Brown is active even on dull days.

| UKBAP: Not listed |
| GB Red List: Least concern |

Widespread resident

Wingspan   Male: 42–48 mm
          Female: 46–52 mm

♂♀

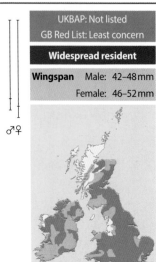

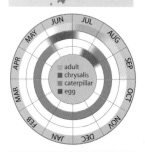

■ adult
■ chrysalis
■ caterpillar
■ egg

WHERE TO LOOK

Generally easy to find anywhere within its range, but look for it in more shaded situations than the Meadow Brown, and especially along the edges of woodlands or along rides. Numbers peak in the third week of July.

LOOK-ALIKES

Meadow Brown (*page 148*)
Gatekeeper (*page 146*)

A widespread and successful species, and one that has been extending its range in both England and Scotland in recent years.

Adult identification: Often confused with the Meadow Brown (*page 148*), from which it is readily separated by the bright, conspicuous, yellow-ringed 'eye' spots on the underside of the wing. The upperwing of a freshly emerged male is almost black, though this fades to brown with age. Females are slightly paler. Look out, too, for the distinctive white fringe to the wings. This species is prone to aberration, which is most noticeable in the 'eye' spots on the underwing ranging from ab. *arete* with tiny white spots to ab. *lanceolata* with large, 'stretched' markings (see *page 36*).

Behaviour: Found in colonies of variable size, some numbering thousands of individuals. The distinctive bobbing flight is rather slow, but often undertaken on dull, cloudy days. Both sexes feed frequently on Bramble and thistle flowers.

Breeding habitat: Tall, lush grasslands, particularly in woodland rides and glades or around scrub and hedgerows. It favours heavy soils, while northern colonies tend to be in more open, less shady areas.

Population and conservation: This species is generally thriving, but tends to suffer badly following drought summers. It is vulnerable to overgrazing and colonies can be encouraged by leaving grass rides and field headlands uncut.

Egg, caterpillar and chrysalis:

EGG (*page 211*): 0·8 mm (w) × 0·9 mm (h); dome-shaped; pale yellow, turning brownish; scattered among coarse-leaved grasses.

CATERPILLAR (*page 218*): 21 mm; pale yellowish-brown, with a dark band along the back.

CHRYSALIS (*page 224*): 11–13 mm; light sepia-brown, with darker markings, turning black before hatching; hidden at the base of grass tussocks.

Foodplants: a range of grasses.

Fresh males are dark, fading with age, but always with smaller 'eye' spots on the upperwing than females.

Bramble and thistle flowers along woodland rides are a favoured nectar source.

Mountain Ringlet   *Erebia epiphron*

| UKBAP: PRIORITY |
| GB Red List: NEAR THREATENED |
| W&C Act: SALE PROHIBITED |

Localized resident

| Wingspan | Male: 28–36 mm |
| | Female: 28–38 mm |

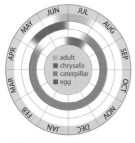

- adult
- chrysalis
- caterpillar
- egg

WHERE TO LOOK

The most accessible site is Ben Lawers in Perthshire, though another reliable Scottish site is Creag Meaghaidh in Inverness-shire. Good sites in the Lake District in Cumbria include Honister, Langdale Pikes and Irton Fell.

LOOK-ALIKES

Scotch Argus (*page 154*)

Our only true mountain butterfly, and restricted to the Scottish Highlands and the Lake District, where its fortunes fluctuate with the weather. It is one of our least-known butterflies.

Adult identification: This brown butterfly is usually found at high altitude. The only other similar species that flies at such altitude is the Scotch Argus (*page 154*). However, the Scotch Argus is larger and brighter, and has distinctive white 'eye' spots on the upperside which Mountain Ringlets lack. In Europe, there are numerous different species of alpine ringlets, all looking rather similar, but here we have just the single species. The orange spots of females are generally slightly larger and lighter than those of males, although the difference can be marginal. Individuals in Scotland (race *scotica*) are slightly larger than those in the Lake District.

Behaviour: A sedentary, colonial species. On sunny days the males can be seen sunbathing or patrolling across their breeding grounds, always remaining close to the ground. Females rarely fly and spend their time egg-laying, basking and nectaring. The lifespan is thought to be short, at the most just a few days.

Breeding habitat: Generally damp mountain grassland at altitudes of 500–700 m in the Lake District, and 350–900 m in Scotland. Scottish colonies favour south-facing slopes, but the Lake District colonies are more adaptable and north-facing slopes are also used.

Population and conservation: Numbers appear to be stable and there may be colonies in the Scottish Highlands that have yet to be discovered. The main threats to this species come from overgrazing and afforestation.

Egg, caterpillar and chrysalis:

EGG (*page 211*): 0·8 mm (w) × 1·2 mm (h); barrel-shaped and ribbed; pale cream at first, becoming darker and mottled and then transparent; laid singly.

CATERPILLAR (*page 218*): 19–20 mm; green with yellowish stripes along the back and along each side.

CHRYSALIS (*page 224*): 10–11 mm; found in a loose cocoon at the base of the foodplant.

Foodplant: Mat-grass (and possibly other grasses).

Mountain Ringlet is much smaller than the Scotch Argus and lacks any 'eye' spots on the upperwing.

It is only worth looking on warm, sunny days, when the males are active.

With a short flight period and colony emergence depending on weather and altitude, this species can be easily overlooked. Try to obtain local information, because flight times vary every year and there will only be a few weeks a year when you can expect to find butterflies on the wing.

Primary habitat is damp grassland: above 350 m and south-facing in Scotland; usually higher in England.

UKBAP: Not listed
GB Red List: Least concern

Localized resident

Wingspan   Male: 44–48 mm
Female: 46–52 mm

♂♀

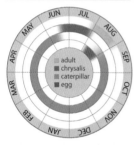

- adult
- chrysalis
- caterpillar
- egg

WHERE TO LOOK

Easy to locate within its Scottish range on sunny days, when it is often the commonest butterfly. Creag Meagaidh in Inverness-shire is a reliable site. The English sites are at Arnside Knott and Smardale Gill in Cumbria.

LOOK-ALIKES

Mountain Ringlet (*page 152*)
Meadow Brown (*page 148*)

Though this butterfly flourishes throughout much of upland Scotland, it has declined in the southernmost parts of its range and can now only be found at two isolated sites in Cumbria. It has also declined elsewhere in Europe.

Adult identification: Most easily confused with the Meadow Brown (*page 148*), but is much darker (the upperwings of freshly emerged males being almost black), while the white 'eye' spots are distinctive. Unlike the Meadow Brown, it only flies when the sun is shining. Also similar to the smaller Mountain Ringlet (*page 152*) but usually found at lower altitudes. Butterflies in England and north west Scotland (race *caledonia*) are slightly larger.

Behaviour: The males are most active in sunshine on windless days, when they will patrol incessantly in search of a mate, and make for cover as soon as the sun disappears. They are active as soon as the sun comes out, even very early in the morning on east-facing slopes. On overcast days, if the temperature is above 15 °C, males may be moderately active. Flying males keep close to the ground, investigating anything that is brown. Females are inconspicuous, basking on sunny days and seldom taking flight.

Breeding habitat: In Scotland, this species is found in damp acid grasslands, around sheltered bogs and in woodland clearings, up to about 500 m. The two English colonies are on sheltered limestone grassland.

Population and conservation: Stable in Scotland, where it is widespread and often abundant, but declining elsewhere in Europe, where it is categorized as near threatened. The chief threats to its survival appear to be overgrazing, agricultural 'improvements' to grassland, and afforestation. The Cumbrian colonies are flourishing, but it has been lost from a number of other sites in northern England.

Egg, caterpillar and chrysalis:

Egg (*page 211*): 1·0 mm (w) ×1·3 mm (h); pale yellow, developing speckles with age. Extremely difficult to find in the wild.

Caterpillar (*page 218*): 27 mm; ochreous, with two whitish lines along each side, the upper edged with brown dashes.

Chrysalis (*page 224*): 13 mm; formed at base of grass tussocks.

Foodplants: a range of grasses, often Purple Moor-grass in Scotland and Blue Moor-grass in England.

M

M

Only active when sunny or warm …

F

F

…sit in a suitable area and wait for the sun.

Typical Scotch Argus habitat.

UKBAP: Priority
GB Red List: Near Threatened
Wildlife (NI) Order: Protected

Abundant resident

♂♀ **Wingspan**   Male: 29 mm
                Female: 34 mm

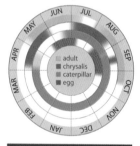

- adult
- chrysalis
- caterpillar
- egg

WHERE TO LOOK

In suitable grassland habitat throughout much of Britain and Ireland. In southern England, adults may be encountered from late April until early October.

LOOK-ALIKES

Large Heath (*page 158*)
'Golden' skippers
  (*pages 42–51*)
At a distance:
Small Copper (*page 104*)

One of our most widespread butterflies, although many colonies have been lost in recent years due to intensive agriculture and changing patterns of land use.

Adult identification: Best identified by a combination of size, colour and behaviour. Its pale, washed-out beige colouring separates it from other brown butterflies, and from the five 'golden' skippers (*pages 42–51*) – though these have a much quicker, darting flight. It is variable in colour, with both bright and dull individuals flying together in the same colony. Butterflies from western Scotland (race *rhoumensis*) are usually the dullest. The size of the 'eye' spots also varies.

Behaviour: Its erratic, low flight is characteristic. Like the Grayling (*page 144*), it virtually never settles with its wings open. It lands with the 'eye' spot of its forewing visible, but soon draws the forewing down behind the hindwing. Males and unmated females congregate in territorial breeding areas where males fight amongst themselves to establish dominance prior to mating. Once mated, females disperse to lay their eggs, and seldom return to the original breeding area. Adults like to sip nectar from low-growing flowering plants, often favouring yellow flowers, such as dandelions and hawkbits.

Breeding habitat: This species favours dry, well-drained grassland, particularly on heathland, downland or coastal dunes, but colonies may also be found in many other situations, from roadside verges to woodland rides. It requires fine-leaved grasses, which are the foodplant of the caterpillar.

Population and conservation: Though this butterfly flourishes where native grasses can be found in abundance, colonies are soon destroyed by so-called grassland 'improvement' and ploughing. Light grazing is beneficial, but overgrazing can destroy the habitat.

Egg, caterpillar and chrysalis:

Egg (*page 211*): 0·5 mm (w) × 0·7 mm (h); almost spherical; pale green, turning off-white and freckled; laid singly on grass blades.

Caterpillar (*page 218*): 20 mm; green, and well camouflaged, with a dark green, white-edged line along the back.

Chrysalis (*page 224*): 8·5 mm; pale-green, usually with black streaking or stripes.

Foodplants: fine-leaved grasses, especially Sheep's-fescue.

The territorial males engage in fights with rivals and are easier to see than the females.

Small Heath very rarely settles with its upperwings on show.

Look for adults nectaring on low-growing yellow flowers.

Any meadow rich in native grasses and with plenty of nectar sources is worth investigating.

| UKBAP: PRIORITY |
| GB Red List: VULNERABLE |
| W&C Act: SALE PROHIBITED |

| **Declining resident** |
| **Wingspan:**   35–40 mm |

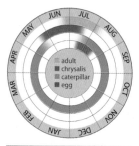

■ adult
■ chrysalis
■ caterpillar
■ egg

WHERE TO LOOK

Bellart How Moss and Meathop Moss in Cumbria for race *davus.*
Allt Mhuic and Creag Meagaidh in Inverness-shire for *scotica.*
Bowness Common and Glasson Moss in Cumbria and Fen Bog in North Yorkshire are good sites for *polydama.*

LOOK-ALIKES

Small Heath (*page 156*)

A butterfly of boggy moorland, which remains widespread over much of Scotland and parts of Ireland but has declined in northern England and Wales.

Adult identification: This is one of our most variable butterflies, with its appearance varying not only in different parts of its range, but also within colonies. Three different races are recognized. In lowland England, the dark race *davus* has clearly defined 'eye' spots. In Scotland, the race *scotica* is paler, with greyish wings that are virtually spotless. In northern England, Wales and Ireland an intermediate race, *polydama*, occurs. This is paler than *davus*, with many, but less pronounced spots. The only butterfly with which this species can be confused is the Small Heath (*page 156*), which is noticeably smaller. However, the two species are rarely found together: the Large Heath is a genuine wetland butterfly, while the Small Heath favours well-drained grassland.

Behaviour: A slow-flying and highly sedentary butterfly that can often be seen fluttering over bogs even on dull days. Like the Grayling (*page 144*), this butterfly never basks with its wings held open, but males will tilt their bodies to warm themselves in the sun.

Breeding habitat: Raised bogs, blanket bogs and acidic moorland, usually below 500 m. Its main requirements are the presence of Hare's-tail Cottongrass, the caterpillar's foodplant, and Cross-leaved Heath, a favourite source of nectar for the adults.

Population and conservation: With its specialized habitat being vulnerable to afforestation, drainage, peat extraction and overgrazing, this is a highly sensitive species. Its future depends on safeguarding peatlands, and ensuring appropriate management.

Egg, caterpillar and chrysalis:

EGG (*page 211*): 0·8 mm (w) × 0·8 mm (h); barrel-shaped; yellow at first, developing dark blotches with age; laid on cottongrasses.
CATERPILLAR (*page 218*): 25 mm; green with a yellow-edged dark green line along the back, and two prominent pale yellow bands along each side.
CHRYSALIS (*page 224*): 11 mm; green with black stripes, though their boldness varies considerably.

Foodplants: cottongrasses, especially Hare's-tail Cottongrass.

▲ The race scotica, with grey, spotless underwing, against its preferred habitat.

The races polydama ▲ and davus ▼ inhabit wet, boggy areas where the larval foodplant, Hare's-tail Cottongrass, and favoured nectar source, Cross-leaved Heath, are found.

Former breeding species and occasional migrants

Cardinal *Argynnis pandora* from southern and south-eastern Europe – two British records but possibly overlooked

This section provides full accounts for the four former breeders, 11 rare migrants and one species with unknown status. There are another six extreme rarities that have been recorded in Britain and Ireland, and these are shown here for completeness, with a summary of the records. Although such rarities do appear in Britain or Ireland naturally, there is always a chance that you may find an unusual butterfly that has escaped or been released from captivity (albeit often illegally – see the section on *Conservation and legislation page 232*); some of these species are shown on *pages 192–193*.

A complete list of the butterflies that are believed to have occurred naturally in the wild in Britain and Ireland can be found on *page 225*.

American Painted Lady
Vanessa virginiensis
– very rare vagrant from the USA.

Apollo *Parnassius apollo*
– while most records are of escapes,
a few are of genuine vagrants from southern Europe.

Large Chequered Skipper
Heteropterus morpheus from Europe
– bred on Jersey *ca.* 1946–1996.

Lang's Short-tailed Blue
Leptotes pirithous from southern Europe – just one record from 1938.

Scarce Swallowtail *Iphiclides podalirius*
– very rare vagrant but widespread in Europe.

The likely origins of the vagrant species that have occurred in Britain or Ireland are shown on the map below. A few of these species (in red text) have bred, or are believed likely to have bred successfully in Britain.

From the East or South-east
Apollo (*opposite*)
Scarce Tortoiseshell (*page 182*)
Camberwell Beauty (*page 186*)

From the West
Monarch (*page 188*)
American Painted Lady (*opposite*)

From the South or South-east
Scarce Swallowtail (*opposite*)
Bath White (*page 164*)
Pale Clouded Yellow (*page 166*)
Berger's Clouded Yellow (*page 166*)
Long-tailed Blue (*page 170*)
Lang's Short-tailed Blue (*opposite*)
Short-tailed Blue (*page 172*)
Queen of Spain Fritillary (*page 180*)
Large Tortoiseshell (*page 184*)
Cardinal (*opposite*)
Large Chequered Skipper (*opposite*)

The following annotations are used on the maps for vagrant, rare migrant and former breeding species (*pages 162–190*):

■ European breeding range
■ Migrant range
➤ Possible direction of movement
● Confirmed record (i = introduction)
● Former breeding area

161

UKBAP: Not assessed
GB Red List: REGIONALLY EXTINCT

Extinct resident

Wingspan: 56–68 mm

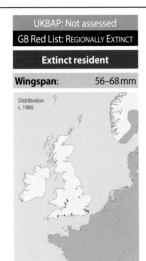

Distribution
c. 1900

This handsome butterfly once had a highly localized distribution in southern England, but became extinct in the 1920s. It remains widely but locally distributed in · continental Europe.

Adult identification: A combination of size and its powerful soaring flight make this an easy butterfly to recognize. Its name perfectly describes what it looks like. When perched, its beautifully veined wings are obvious and unmistakable.

Behaviour: A colonial species whose numbers tend to fluctuate wildly from year to year. Adults start the day by basking in the sun, before venturing out into the surrounding countryside. Both sexes spend much time feeding, when they are tame and readily approachable. There is one generation a year, caterpillars hibernating from September to early May, with adults on the wing from June to early August. In hot weather, butterflies will sometimes settle on damp ground to absorb moisture from the surface

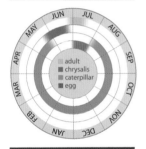

Breeding habitat: Scrub, woodland edge, flowery meadows, orchards, hay fields, and roadside verges.

Status: Despite many attempts to re-establish this species in England, including one by Winston Churchill at Chartwell in Kent, all have eventually failed. It remains widespread in continental Europe, although it has declined in many countries.

WHERE TO LOOK

Former strongholds were in southern England, although its range extended as far north as Yorkshire. It can still be found easily in continental Europe, often in large numbers.

LOOK-ALIKES

Large White (*page 62*)
Green-veined White (*page 66*)
Small White (*page 64*)
Marbled White (*page 138*)

Egg, caterpillar and chrysalis:

EGG (*page 207*): 0·5 mm (w) × 1·0 mm (h); bottle-shaped and ribbed like other white butterflies; primrose yellow when laid, turning grey over time; laid in batches of a hundred or so on the leaves of the foodplant.

CATERPILLAR (*page 213*): 38 mm; black with a broken ochre-coloured stripe on each flank and a grey underside.

CHRYSALIS (*page 219*): 25 mm; Variable, reflecting the location where it was formed, usually greenish-yellow spotted with black.

Foodplants: Blackthorn, Hawthorn and, sometimes, cultivated fruit trees.

In southern France, butterflies are on the wing from May to early August; June is probably the best month to look.

Typical European Black-veined White habitat.

UKBAP: Not assessed
GB Red List: Not assessed

Rare migrant

Wingspan: 38–48 mm

WHERE TO LOOK

You could be lucky enough to come across one during high summer anywhere in southern England, most likely in meadows, dry grasslands, coastal dunes and waste ground, but only during an irruption year, when hundreds may move northwards, emanating from southern Europe

LOOK-ALIKES

Green-veined White (*page 66*)
Small White (*page 64*)
Female Orange-tip (*page 68*)
Marbled White (*page 138*)

A very rare visitor to southern England, where it may have bred in the past.

Adult identification: In flight, this species can easily be mistaken for a Green-veined (*page 66*) or Small White (*page 64*), despite its more purposeful flight. At rest, the mottled pattern and colour of the underside of the hindwing is easily confused with the female Orange-tip (*page 68*), although during the spring flight period of this species the Bath White is highly unlikely to be encountered in England. When seen well, the black-and-white chequering of the upper wing-tips is diagnostic.

Behaviour: A very mobile species, often flying great distances.

Breeding habitat: Adults can be seen almost anywhere, often found on derelict, disturbed ground or rough land and roadside verges.

Status: In 1945 there was an exceptional immigration to southern England in July and early August, and the species almost certainly bred. Subsequent records have been few. It is essentially a Mediterranean butterfly, but migrates northwards every year, colonizing new areas, breeding for a few generations and then usually dying out as it is generally unable to survive northern European winters.

Egg, caterpillar and chrysalis:

Egg (*page 207*): 0·4 mm (w) × 0·85 mm (h); bottle-shaped; initially yellowish-green, turning orange before hatching; laid on the leaves of their foodplant.

Caterpillar (*page 212*): 25 mm; initially reddish-brown but changing to lilac-green with fine black dots and longitudinal yellow stripes along its back and sides.

Chrysalis (*page 219*): 19 mm; colour varies from green to brown when formed but matures to pale grey with darker markings; attached to the stalk of a foodplant by a silken girdle.

Foodplants: Wild Mignonette and various plants of the mustard family

Reminiscent of a female Orange-tip, but differs in the chequered pattern on the upperwing.

Mid-July is the most likely time of year to come across this exceedingly rare irruptive migrant.

Rough land and roadside verges are favoured habitats in continental Europe.

Pale Clouded Yellow
Berger's Clouded Yellow

Colias hyale
Colias alfacariensis

×1½

UKBAP: Not assessed
GB Red List: Not assessed

Rare migrants

Wingspan   Male: 33 mm
           Female: 37 mm

♂♀

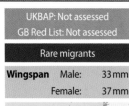

Pale
Clouded
Yellow

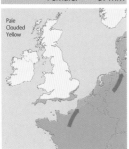

Berger's
Clouded
Yellow

Occasional migrants that are unable to survive the winter here. They are virtually indistinguishable in flight, though the caterpillars look different and have different foodplants.

Adult identification: These two species cannot be readily separated in the field. In comparison with Clouded Yellow (*page 58*), male Pale Clouded Yellows are lemon yellow rather than orange and have thinner black edges to the upperside of their hindwings. Male Berger's are usually more intensely coloured, the orange spot on their hindwing being brighter than in Pale Clouded Yellow, but otherwise they are similar. Females of both species are almost white, and very similar to the pale *helice* form of the Clouded Yellow except that the upperside of their hindwings lacks the grey suffusion. This confusion is made more difficult because significant colour variations occur.

Behaviour: The three species of clouded yellow always land with their wings shut. Berger's Clouded Yellows are usually more active than Pale Clouded Yellows, although they are thought to be less likely to migrate any distance.

Breeding habitat: Berger's Clouded Yellow is more likely to be found on open chalk downland than Pale Clouded Yellow, due to its choice of foodplant. The latter species is more catholic in its choice of habitat, but is typically found in cultivated meadows where Lucerne and clovers can be found. Both species may be found nectaring in flowery meadows.

WHERE TO LOOK

Pale Clouded Yellow is most likely to be found in clover-rich meadows close to the Channel coast of southern England; **Berger's Clouded Yellow** on downland, or cliff tops in Kent and Sussex where Horseshoe Vetch is found. Both are generally seen in August or early September

LOOK-ALIKES

Clouded Yellow (*page 58*)

Status: Pale Clouded Yellow is an occasional migrant to southern England, while Berger's Clouded Yellow is thought to arrive less frequently. However, owing to the similarity between the two species and the *helice* form of Clouded Yellow, their status is uncertain.

Egg, caterpillar and chrysalis:
Egg (*page 207*): 0·4 mm (w) × approx. 1·0 mm (h); bottle-shaped; white turning orange; laid singly.
Caterpillar (*page 212*): 32 mm. **Pale Clouded Yellow:** pale green, finely speckled with black, and with a white stripe with a broken red thread running through it on the sides.
Berger's Clouded Yellow: green with rectangular black spots and yellow stripes along the back and sides.
Chrysalis (*page 219*): 22 mm; predominantly green with longitudinal yellow markings, very similar in colouring and appearance to each other and to that of Clouded Yellow.

Foodplants: Pale Clouded Yellow: clovers or Lucerne; **Berger's Clouded Yellow**: Horseshoe Vetch.

▲ Pale Clouded Yellow

Berger's Clouded Yellow ▼

▼ Clouded yellow uppersides normally only seen in flight – a good view is essential to identification.

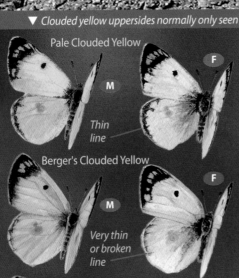

Pale Clouded Yellow

M

F

Thin line

Berger's Clouded Yellow

M

F

Very thin or broken line

Clouded Yellow

F

F f. helice

Thick line

F f. helice

Female Clouded Yellows for comparison ▲▼

UKBAP: Not assessed	
GB Red List: REGIONALLY EXTINCT	
W&C Act: FULL PROTECTION	
EU Habs Dir: (ANN II, ANN IV)	
Bern Convention: (APP II)	
Extinct resident	

Wingspan   Male: 44–58 mm
                    Female: 46–52 mm

♂♀

Distribution
pre 1940

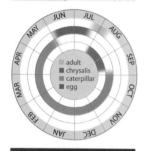

- adult
- chrysalis
- caterpillar
- egg

WHERE TO LOOK

Last seen in Britain at Woodwalton Fen in Cambridgeshire, but this site is now thought to be too small to support a viable population. Dutch butterflies can be seen at the De Weerribben National Park, NE of Amsterdam.

LOOK-ALIKES

Small Copper (*page 104*)

This striking butterfly has been extinct in Britain for over 150 years. Reintroductions were attempted until the early 1990s but all eventually failed.

Adult identification: A stunningly eye-catching butterfly, both sexes readily identified by the brilliant copper-coloured wings that flash as they catch the sun. The male's wings are almost unmarked except for a black margin on the upperside; the female is larger and much more heavily marked.
The undersides of both sexes are similar, the forewing being orange with black spots and the hindwing silvery-grey with a blue suffusion and a prominent orange band near the rear margin. It is readily told from the Small Copper (*page 104*) by its larger size and, in the case of the male, its unmarked copper upperwings.

Behaviour: Lives in small colonies and only active on bright, sunny days. It is less pugnacious and territorial than the Small Copper.

Breeding habitat: Extensive areas of open fen where Water Dock flourishes. Curiously, with the exception of the Dutch population, this species has two broods a year in continental Europe, instead of one, and their caterpillars feed on several different species of dock.

Status: Always rare in England, its final extinction was due to the destruction of the extensive fenland habitat it requires. There are hopes that habitat management in the Norfolk Broads may one day allow this species to be reintroduced successfully, using stock from Holland, where the rare single-brooded form survives. Elsewhere in Europe, the double-brooded race is locally common.

Egg, caterpillar and chrysalis:
EGG (*opposite, top inset*): 0.65 mm (w) × 0.4 mm (h); crown-shaped disc; white; laid singly on the leaves of the foodplant.
CATERPILLAR (*opposite, centre inset*): 20 mm; grub-like; green but darker along its back and between adjacent segments.
CHRYSALIS (*opposite, bottom inset*): 11 mm; initially green turning a variegated ash colour; formed on the stem of the foodplant.

Foodplant: Water Dock (this is the sole foodplant of the Dutch race which is similar to the extinct British race).

Although the female is similar to a large Small Copper, the upperside of the male is umistakable.

The British race was single-brooded, flying in July and August.

Extensive areas of open fen with plentiful Water Dock are the exclusive habitat.

Long-tailed Blue
Lampides boeticus

UKBAP: Not assessed
GB Red List: Not assessed

Rare migrant

Wingspan   Male: 32–34 mm
Female: 36–42 mm

♂♀

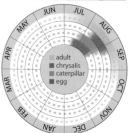

adult
chrysalis
caterpillar
egg

WHERE TO LOOK

Migrants most often appear in gardens along the south coast or on downland with other blues, although have been seen a considerable distance inland. There are records from early July but best looked for in August and September in hot, open habitats where the foodplants grow.

LOOK-ALIKES

Purple Hairstreak (*page 84*)
Common Blue (*page 96*)
Adonis Blue (*page 98*)
Chalkhill Blue (*page 100*)

A migratory butterfly that is a rare and irregular visitor to southern England, usually in late summer.

Adult identification: Most easily identified by the distinctive 'tails' on the trailing edge of the hindwing (though these can become broken), with two adjacent black spots. Look also for the distinctive white striping on the underside of both the hindwings and forewings. The upperside of the male is violet-blue, while the female is predominantly brown with variable amounts of blue scales.

Behaviour: A fast-flying butterfly, with a rapid and jerky flight, similar to that of a hairstreak.

Breeding habitat: In continental Europe, most often found in flower-rich meadows where members of the pea family grow. Most British records have been in gardens, or on downland in the southern third of England.

Status: A highly successful and widespread species in continental Europe, and often abundant within its range. It breeds all the year round and so permanent colonies are almost certainly confined to the Mediterranean zone. It is a highly migratory butterfly that often migrates north, but rarely crosses the English Channel. The British climate is normally too cool for it to become established here. In 2013, there were sightings at nine sites from Suffolk to Devon. Some bred successfully, but their offspring did not survive the winter.

Egg, caterpillar and chrysalis:
EGG (*page 208*): 0·5 mm (w) × approx. 0·3 mm (h); flattened sphere; creamy-white.
CATERPILLAR (*page 215*): 15 mm; green or reddish-brown, with a dark stripe along its back and whitish lines each side.
CHRYSALIS (*page 221*): 12 mm; yellowish-pink with brown blotches, becoming cream-coloured with age.

Foodplants: Bladder-senna, Broad-leaved and Narrow-leaved Everlasting-peas, Broom and Mange-tout pea. Caterpillars are sometimes found on imported peas or beans.

The distinctive 'tails', striped underwing and jerky flight are reminiscent of Purple Hairstreak.

Almost annual in recent years, most sightings have been in August and September.

Long-tailed Blue in typical habitat.

Short-tailed Blue *Everes argiades*

(Bloxworth Blue)

UKBAP: Not assessed
GB Red List: Not assessed

Rare vagrant

Wingspan: 20–30 mm

WHERE TO LOOK

Should this species occur in Britain, which, at present, is unlikely, possible locations would be clover-rich fields along the south coast. Try searching in July–September after periods of southerly winds.

LOOK-ALIKES

Common Blue (*page 96*)
Small Blue (*page 88*)
Holly Blue (*page 86*)
Silver-studded Blue (*page 94*)

An extremely rare vagrant to southern England. The first British specimens were recorded in 1885 at Bloxworth Heath in Dorset, hence its alternative English name.

Adult identification: One of a number of similar species that occur in Europe. The tails are tiny but distinctive. Look also for the twin orange spots near the tail on the silvery underside, which separates this from all the other blues, including the other short-tailed blues that occur in continental Europe. The male has violet-blue wings with black margins, which in bright sunlight contrast in flight with the pale underwings. The female is dark brown with a variable scattering of purple scales, usually near the base of the wings.

Behaviour: Unlike the Long-tailed Blue (*page 170*), this is not a migratory species, only rarely wandering to southern England. In continental Europe, it is most active in the early morning and late afternoon, resting during the heat of the day.

Breeding habitat: Woodland edges, unimproved grassland and heaths.

Status: Very occasionally recorded as an adult in Britain. This butterfly can be found right across Europe from northern Spain eastwards but it is a localized species and may be hard to find. Although it is rare in northern France, if we have warmer summers it could potentially colonize southern England as it utilizes a range of foodplants that are common here.

Egg, caterpillar and chrysalis:

EGG (*page 208*): approx. 0·45 mm (w) × 0·2 mm (h); squashed sphere with fine surface reticulations; creamy-white.

CATERPILLAR (*page 215*): 9–10 mm; pale green with a darker stripe along its back and broken green stripes along each side.

CHRYSALIS (*page 221*): approx. 8 mm; hairy; pale green with some minute black markings.

Foodplants: a range of species in the pea family, including Common Bird's-foot-trefoil, Red Clover and Tufted Vetch.

A potential colonist, any blue with tiny 'tails' warrants investigation!

There are two or three broods and usually the later broods are larger, so July-September is the best time to look.

Flower-rich unimproved grassland is preferred.

× 1½ # Mazarine Blue

Cyaniris semiargus

| UKBAP: Not assessed |
| GB Red List: REGIONALLY EXTINCT |
| **Extinct resident/vagrant** |

Wingspan Male: 32–36mm
Female: 34–38mm

♂♀

Distribution
pre 1900

WHERE TO LOOK

Unless action is taken to attempt a reintroduction, there is little chance of seeing this species in Britain. Try searching fields with Red Clover in June and July, the months when there have been most records of migrants.

LOOK-ALIKES

Common Blue (*page 96*)
Silver-studded Blue (*page 94*)
Holly Blue (*page 86*)

An attractive, medium-sized blue, similar in size to the Common Blue but with no orange markings on its underwings. It formerly bred in England but became extinct around 1903; it is now only a very rare visitor.

Adult identification: The upperside of the male is a dull purplish-blue; the female is brown. Both sexes have white edges to their wings, the male having a dark margin along the inside of the white border. The underside of both sexes is a pale cinnamon-grey colour, with a blue tinge near the body and a few black spots encircled with white. Only the Silver-studded Blue (*page 94*) has a similar upperwing colouration but it is smaller and distinguished by the silver-blue studs at the edge of the underside of its hindwings.

Behaviour: Lives in discrete colonies in continental Europe and is generally non-migratory. Eggs are laid on the flowerheads of clover and newly-hatched caterpillars bore into and eat the flowers. If there is only one brood, they hibernate and then resume feeding on new shoots the following spring. Their interaction with ants is not understood, but it is known that ants are attracted to both the caterpillars and their chrysalises.

Breeding habitat: Unimproved pasture and hay meadows where its foodplant occurs.

Status: Now extinct in Britain. The few records of genuine immigrants have come from the south coast of England. Little is known about this butterfly's former distribution and the reasons for its extinction.

Egg, caterpillar and chrysalis:

EGG (*page 208*): 0·55 mm (w) × 0·3 mm (h); flattened sphere, with a finely-ribbed surface; white.

CATERPILLAR (*page 215*): 10 mm; yellowish-green with darker lines on its back and sides and covered in fine hairs.

CHRYSALIS (*page 221*): 9 mm; pale olive-green, turning olive-brown; formed close to the foodplant.

Foodplant: mainly Red Clover.

Any medium-sized blue that lacks orange spots on the underwing is worth a closer look.

Generally non-migratory but there are a few records of presumed migrants on the south coast in June/July.

Typical European Mazarine Blue habitat.

Geranium Bronze

Cacyreus marshalli

UKBAP: Not assessed
GB Red List: Not assessed

Accidental introduction

♂♀ **Wingspan** Male: 15–23 mm
Female: 18–27 mm

WHERE TO LOOK

The first British record was in Lewes, East Sussex in 1997. Subsequently, there have been sightings in several different parts of the country, all believed to be come from imported *Pelargonium* plants.

LOOK-ALIKES

Female blues (*pages 86–101*)
Hairstreaks (*pages 76–85*)

A southern African species, now firmly established in several Mediterranean countries, and recently recorded in England after being introduced on imported *Pelargoniums*.

Adult identification: Tiny. Look for the distinctive 'tails' on the hindwings, and the chequered white fringe to the upperside of both the forewings and hindwings, which are, indeed, bronze-coloured. The undersides of each of the wings are heavily patterned. There is no other native species that this butterfly can be confused with. Both sexes are the same, the female being slightly larger.

Behaviour: A weak-flying species, usually found close to its foodplant. It first succeeded in colonizing the Balearic Islands, and then coastal Mediterranean Spain, as a result of being accidentally imported (probably as caterpillars) on *Pelargonium* plants. It makes very short, jerky flights, often returning to its point of departure.

Breeding habitat: In Europe, it depends on cultivated *Pelargonium* species, so is invariably found in gardens, window boxes or wherever its foodplants can be found. The young caterpillars burrow into developing flower buds, before moving outside as they mature to eat the plant's leaves. This is a continuously-brooded species which requires warm winters for its survival, so is unlikely to become established in Britain unless on indoor plants.

Status: An unwelcome colonist in the Mediterranean, where its caterpillar's liking for the flowers, leaves and stems of *Pelargoniums* has made it unpopular with gardeners. It has already proved to be a serious pest in the horticultural trade and is designated as a 'pest species'. Sightings in the UK should be reported to the Plant Health Service (see *page 235*).

Egg, caterpillar and chrysalis (*opposite*):
EGG: 0·5 mm (w) × 0·3 mm (h); disc-shaped; white; laid singly on flower buds or the underside of leaves of the foodplant.
CATERPILLAR: 9 mm; green, with a variable pink stripe with white edges along its back and each side; covered with tiny white hairs.
CHRYSALIS: 13 mm; ochreous-brown, speckled with minute brown spots, and covered in fine white hairs; attached either to the host plant or in leaf-litter on the ground.

Note: The lower images of the male, female and early life stages opposite are those of the 1997 Lewes record

Foodplants: cultivated *Pelargonium* plants.

The combination of bronze colouration, 'tails' and underside pattern is unlike any of the native species.

Pelargoniums *with heavy leaf damage may indicate that this species is present.*

Only likely to be encountered on or close to cultivated Pelargonium plants.

| UKBAP: Not assessed |
| GB Red List: Not assessed |
| Rare migrant |
| **Wingspan** Spring: 30–40 mm |
| Summer: 34–46 mm |
| (Females slightly larger than males) |

Sp Su

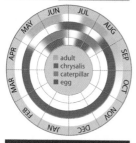

adult
chrysalis
caterpillar
egg

WHERE TO LOOK

The east and south coasts are likely to be the most likely areas for migrants to turn up.

LOOK-ALIKES

Unmistakable!

A colony was introduced into the Forest of Dean in 1912, but later failed or was destroyed. Subsequently, there have been occasional sightings at various localities, thought to have been captive-bred butterflies. However, the increasing range of this migratory species in Europe suggests that colonization could begin before long, either by butterflies that have arrived naturally, or following the accidental release of captive-bred stock.

Adult identification: This is an unusual species because the uppersides of spring butterflies have the distinct look of a fritillary (*pages 108–123*), while summer butterflies look more like White Admirals (*page 124*). The undersides of adults from both broods are similar, except that summer brood butterflies have more white than those that have passed the winter as a chrysalis. In both broods, prominent white veins on their undersides look like connecting roads radiating outwards from a central location at the butterfly's thorax.

Behaviour: In sunny weather, Maps will spend a lot of time basking with their wings open. They tend to fly short distances, often gliding, before returning to their starting point. They are on the wing between April and October.

Breeding habitat: Uses a range of habitats, often preferring moist woodland edges, but also spreading to open country including gardens and parkland. It normally has two generations a year, but may sometimes have a third generation if the summer is very hot.

Status: Maps are found in much of France and Germany and eastwards into Russia. The Netherlands was colonized progressively from about 1960, with the species gradually spreading northwards.

Egg, caterpillar and chrysalis:
Egg: (*pages 210, 211*): dimensions not recorded; pale-green, ribbed, laid on the underside of nettles in chains of up to a dozen eggs, hanging down like a catkin.
Caterpillar: (*page 216*): 20 mm; lives in colonies; mature caterpillars are very dark brown with lighter-coloured prickly spines and with two black 'horns' on their black heads.
Chrysalis: (*page 222*): dimensions not recorded; dark greyish-brown, with lighter points, and with a purplish tinge; attached to the foodplant.

Foodplant: Common Nettle, Small Nettle.

Females are often slightly larger than males, with shorter, more rounded abdomens.

The underside markings of the summer brood are more extensively white.

▲▼ *Spring brood f. levana*

Summer brood brood f. prorsa ▲▼

There is a significant difference in size and upperside pattern between the two broods.

Although the Map usually occurs in colonies, individuals (particularly of the summer generation) may disperse widely and can sometimes be found in gardens.

Queen of Spain Fritillary   *Issoria (Argynnis) lathonia*

Rare migrant

Wingspan Male: 34–52 mm
Female: 50–56 mm

♂♀

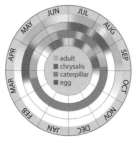

adult
chrysalis
caterpillar
egg

WHERE TO LOOK

Along the south and east coasts of England in the autumn, though don't expect success! The best places to look vary from year to year depending on the prevailing weather conditions.

LOOK-ALIKES

Dark Green Fritillary (*page 120*)
Silver-washed Fritillary
(*page 122*)
Comma (*page 136*)

A rare migrant from the near-continent. It occasionally breeds, but the offspring rarely survive the British winter.

Adult identification: The distinctive wing shape and fast, powerful flight give this species a totally different jizz from any of our other fritillaries. The best distinguishing marks are the large silver patches on the underside of the hindwings, which are the same for both sexes. The female is larger than the male, with more green at the base of its upperwings.

Behaviour: A low-flying, sun-loving species that often stops to bask in the sun, usually on patches of bare ground where it will perch with wings held open in a wide 'V'. Though a strong flyer, there is a slight jerkiness that is reminiscent of the Wall (*page 142*). This species lives in residential colonies in continental Europe, from which some individuals may wander considerable distances.

Breeding habitat: In continental Europe, it favours dry limestone areas, heathland and sand dunes where its favoured foodplant, the Field Pansy, grows commonly. The nearest colonies to Britain are in The Netherlands, in dunes along the North Sea coast.

Status: Widely distributed and quite common in continental Europe, but a rare migrant to Britain, where it can be encountered anywhere along the south and east coast, especially in the autumn. There have been breeding records but the caterpillars are unlikely to be able to survive a hard winter. In the late 1990s, there were a number of records on the Suffolk coast that suggested a small breeding colony might have become established, but this later disappeared.

Egg, caterpillar and chrysalis:
EGG: approx. 0·6 mm (w) × 0·7 mm (h); like a conical barrel with axial ribs; pale yellow initially, becoming darker; laid singly.
CATERPILLAR (*page 216*): 32 mm; variable, usually velvety black with white longitudinal stripes and brownish spines.
CHRYSALIS (*page 222*): 17–19 mm; very dark brown with white markings, resembling a bird's dropping.

Foodplants: probably Wild Pansy or Field Pansy, although many species of violets are used in continental Europe.

The very large silver patches that predominate the underside of the hindwing are unlike any other British fritillary.

Almost annual, adults are normally encountered in southern England especially in September and October.

The sun-loving Queen of Spain Fritillary frequently basks on open ground.

×1½ **Scarce Tortoiseshell** *Nymphalis xanthomelas*

(Yellow-legged Tortoiseshell)

UKBAP: Not assessed
GB Red List: Not assessed

Rare migrant

Wingspan   Male: 55–60mm
Female: 66–71mm

♂♀

WHERE TO LOOK

The east coast from Lincolnshire to Kent is where wanderers were seen in 2014. Watch for advance warning of migratory movements in continental Europe, particularly the arrival of migrants into The Netherlands in mid-summer – then examine buddleia bushes.

LOOK-ALIKES

Large Tortoiseshell (*page 184*)
Small Tortoiseshell (*page 132*)
Comma (*page 136*)

Only recorded once in Britain, in 1953, until six or seven individuals were sighted in different places in south-east England in July 2014, mainly near the coast.

Adult Identification: Key features that separate Scarce Tortoiseshells from Large Tortoiseshells (*page 184*) are (i) white rather than yellow markings at the apex of each upper forewing, (ii) broader black marginal borders to the upperwings that fade gradually towards their inner edges, (iii) the absence of lighter markings on the inside edges of these borders, (iv) lighter coloured legs. To be certain of identification, you need to look for all these characteristics. Leg colour is particularly difficult to judge because it depends greatly on lighting and camera position. The alternative name of Yellow-legged Tortoiseshell implies greater colour difference from the other two tortoiseshell species than is really the case. When freshly emerged, the orange-brown base colour of Scarce Tortoiseshells is deeper than that of Large Tortoiseshells. Note that Small Tortoiseshells (*page 132*) also have a white spot near the apex of each forewing.

Behaviour: Like all tortoiseshells, this is a strong, fast flier, only stopping occasionally to nectar or bask in the sun. The flight period is generally two or three weeks during July to September, after which the adult hibernates, reappearing the next spring.

Breeding habitat: As is the case with Large Tortoiseshell, Scarce Tortoiseshell is associated with the edges of deciduous woodland, particularly damp woodland and lake and river margins where its caterpillars' foodplants – willows and poplars – are abundant. Similarly, Scarce Tortoiseshells are strongly attracted by willow blossom after they emerge from hibernation.

Status: This species is known to have a strong migratory tendency and can fly long distances, but it is rarely seen west of a line from the Baltic to the Adriatic. Occasional migrants are found in Finland and southern Sweden, from where those seen in the UK during a ten-day period in 2014 are thought to have originated. These individuals were probably outliers from a migrant stream swept down by north-easterly winds.

Egg, caterpillar and chrysalis:
EGG: 0·6mm (w) × 0·8mm (h); similar to the Large Tortoiseshell (*pages 210, 211*), laid in batches on twigs.
CATERPILLAR (*page 217*): 45mm; lives in groups in conspicuous silken tents; mature caterpillars are black and yellow with branching black spines.
CHRYSALIS: 27mm; very similar to that of the Large Tortoiseshell (*page 223*), suspended from the foodplant.

Foodplant: usually willows and poplars.

Large Tortoiseshell
– no white mark,
narrow border

Scarce Tortoiseshell
– white mark, broad border

Small Tortoiseshell
– much smaller,
three spots on forewing

Ad

Scarce Tortoiseshell differs from the Large Tortoiseshell by having a white spot on its forewing.

Ad

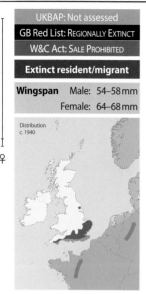

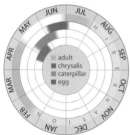

UKBAP: Not assessed
GB Red List: REGIONALLY EXTINCT
W&C Act: SALE PROHIBITED

Extinct resident/migrant

Wingspan Male: 54–58 mm
Female: 64–68 mm

Distribution
c.1940

♂♀

adult
chrysalis
caterpillar
egg

WHERE TO LOOK

Though its stronghold was southern England, this butterfly once occurred in the Midlands, and has been recorded from both Scotland and Wales. It is still common in France and much of continental Europe.

LOOK-ALIKES

Small Tortoiseshell (*page 132*)
Scarce Tortoiseshell (*page 182*)
Comma (*page 136*)

Now almost certainly extinct as a breeding species in Britain, the few sightings every year most likely being of released individuals or sporadic migrants.

Adult identification: This species resembles the Small Tortoiseshell (*page 132*) but is slightly larger and duller. The best way to tell the two apart is the complete absence of a white spot in the corner of the Large Tortoiseshell's forewing. It also resembles the similar-sized Scarce Tortoiseshell, which can be differentiated using a suite of features – see *page 182* for details. Males and females look the same.

Behaviour: A fast, strong flier. After emerging, adults fly for only a few weeks in June and July before hibernating, seeking out cracks or holes in tree trunks. They re-appear the following spring, when they can be found basking, with wings held wide apart, on tree trunks that have been warmed by the sun. Mating takes place in the spring, and by the beginning of May few, if any, adults survive.

Breeding habitat: A butterfly that favours the edge of deciduous woodlands, but can also be found in well-wooded hedgerows and wooded lanes. Emerging adults like to feed on willow blossom, so favoured woodlands usually have an abundance of these tree species. Adults also visit field and garden flowers, favouring wild thistles.

Status: Though it is often suggested that migrants from continental Europe reach southern England, these seem to be so infrequent that there is little chance of this species re-establishing itself naturally in Britain. Its population has risen and fallen in the past, but its last period of relative abundance in England was 1945–48. Many recent sightings have been traced to releases of captive stock, but the numerous occasional sightings along the south and east coast of England are probably genuine migrants.

Egg, caterpillar and chrysalis:
EGG: (*pages 210, 211*): 0·6 mm (w) × 0·8 mm (h); yellow, becoming darker with age; laid in batches encircling twigs of the foodplant.
CATERPILLAR (*page 217*): 40 mm; black, with minute white spots and an orange stripe on either side, and with orange-brown spines; gregarious, feeding on young leaves of their host tree and sheltering on or beneath an obvious silken web.
CHRYSALIS (*page 223*): 27 mm; variable in colour, but usually well camouflaged to resemble tree bark where it is formed.

Foodplants: usually elms or willows.

Small Tortoiseshell

Large Tortoisehell lacks the white spot on the forewing shown by the Small Tortoiseshell.

In southern France, hibernating adults can emerge as early as February and fly until May. Their offspring are on the wing in June and July but, before the end of July, they have usually gone into hibernation, where they remain for the rest of the year.

Camberwell Beauty

Nymphalis antiopa

UKBAP: Not assessed
GB Red List: Not assessed

Annual migrant

Wingspan Male: 76–86 mm
Female: 78–88 mm

♂♀

A rare but regular vagrant from continental Europe and Scandinavia, although never recorded breeding in Britain.

Adult identification: Readily identified by its large size, deep chocolate-brown wings fringed with pale yellow (sometimes almost white) borders, and a line of blue dots edging these margins. The underside is dark, except for a pale margin. This is a long-lived species, and towards the end of the flight period specimens are often very tatty and faded.

Behaviour: Its powerful flight is similar to that of a Red Admiral (*page 128*) and, like that species, it will readily visit gardens to feed on buddleias. This species hibernates as an adult, going into hibernation early, usually in August. The adults emerge in early spring the following year and it seems likely that spring records in Britain are of individuals that have overwintered successfully.

WHERE TO LOOK

On buddleias in late summer and early autumn. May be found almost anywhere in the UK, although there is a bias towards East Anglia and south-east England.

LOOK-ALIKES

Red Admiral (*page 128*)
Peacock (*page 134*)

Breeding habitat: In Scandinavia and continental Europe, this butterfly is usually found in or near woodland. Sightings in Britain have come from a variety of habitats, including sand dunes, parks and gardens, especially involving individuals feeding on buddleias. The first British records were of two seen in Camberwell, south London, in 1748.

Status: A widespread species in continental Europe, with migrants recorded annually in Britain. Exceptional influxes occur occasionally, such as in 1976 and 1995 when over 300 individuals were reported on both occasions.

Egg, caterpillar and chrysalis:

EGG: approx. 0·7 mm (w) × 0·9 mm (h); initially yellow but gradually changing through red-brown to a lead-grey tint; laid in large batches on twigs or stems of the host tree in late spring.
CATERPILLAR (*page 217*): 50 mm; velvety black with long black spines and sprinkled with fine white dots and a series of rust-red markings on its back; lives in conspicuous groups on their foodplants.
CHRYSALIS (*page 223*): 25–32 mm; pinkish-brown with the points on the body tipped with orange.

Foodplants: willow, birch, poplar and elm.

A few spring records point to successful overwintering; butterflies can be difficult to spot amongst leafless branches.

Unmistakable, usually encountered from July onwards.

Ad

Often seen feeding on over-ripe fruit.

Ad

Monarch

Danaus plexippus

Wingspan: 105–112 mm

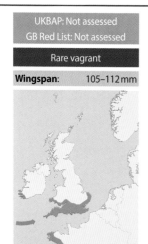

WHERE TO LOOK

In areas rich with nectar plants, including gardens, particularly in Cornwall and the Scilly Islands, and usually near the coast. It can often be seen feeding on Buddleia.

LOOK-ALIKES

Unmistakable!

A rare but spectacular vagrant from North America, especially to south-west Britain and Ireland in the Autumn

Adult identification: Unmistakable. The combination of its large size (much the largest butterfly to occur naturally in Britain and Ireland) and its conspicuous and distinctive colouring ensures that the Monarch can be recognized instantly, even by people with little knowledge of butterflies. The male and female are very similar, except for the males small sex-brand on the hindwings, and both have the same stately, almost bird-like flight.

Behaviour: A very strong flyer, most likely to be seen soaring rapidly, searching for nectar plants. When feeding it can be very approachable.

Breeding habitat: In North America, this species is found in a wide range of habitats, including flowery meadows, pasture, wasteland and gardens. The caterpillars feed on plants of milkweed species that are not native to Britain, so they do not breed here. Vagrants are only occasionally seen in Britain or Ireland, most probably having flown, wind-assisted, from North America, though it is possible that some originate from the Atlantic Macaronesian islands (where they have become established on the Canary Islands and Madeira). Vagrants are generally found close to the coast, often in gardens.

Status: A highly migratory and long-lived butterfly that is widespread in North America. Most records of the species in Britain and Ireland are in September and October, particularly following fast-moving Atlantic depressions. Monarchs are seen somewhere in Britain virtually every year, though the record was in 1999 when over 300 individuals were recorded.

Egg, caterpillar and chrysalis:
Egg (*page 208*): approx. 0·8 mm (w) × 1·2 mm (h); heavily-ribbed; pale yellow; laid singly on the leaves of the foodplant.
Caterpillar (*page 213*): 56 mm; as unmistakable as the adult, striped light green with black and yellow rings and with two thin black filaments extending from segments at both ends.
Chrysalis (*page 224*): 11 mm (w) × 22 mm (h); shining dull-green with white markings and some black spotting, hanging from a leaf or stalk.

Foodplants: milkweeds.

Very large, unmistakable and perhaps the ultimate prize for butterfly-watchers.

September and October are the most likely months In Britain or Ireland, after stormy depressions have crossed the Atlantic. Internet sites for birders often record sightings and alert enthusiasts.

Arran Brown *Erebia ligea*

UKBAP: Not assessed
GB Red List: Not assessed

Extinct resident?/migrant

Wingspan: 48–54 mm

WHERE TO LOOK

The only suggestion is to visit Rannoch Moor or woodland clearings above 1,000 m in the vicinity. But many others have already done this without success, so the chances of success are infinitesimal!

LOOK-ALIKES

Scotch Argus (*page 154*)

Reputedly discovered on the Isle of Arran in 1803. Although common on high ground in continental Europe, it has only been seen very occasionally in Scotland.

Adult identification: This species resembles the Scotch Argus (*page 154*) except for its chequered brown-and-white fringes and a jagged white stripe on the underside of its hindwings, which is usually broader and longer in the female. In the male this border can be thin or virtually absent.

Behaviour: A summer mountain butterfly in Europe from the south of France eastwards, and in Scandinavia. It has one brood a year, with eggs remaining dormant over the winter and hatching in May. Caterpillars later hibernate before pupating in the following spring. Adults will often bask with their wings open.

Breeding habitat: Sheltered, damp, grassy woodland clearings and margins, on high ground, to an altitude of about 1,800 m in continental Europe.

Status: Extinct in Britain. This is another of those cases where English names for butterflies have stuck even though the species in question has been extinct for many years. The original discovery on the Isle of Arran has been debated for years, and there have been other disputed sightings in Scotland. However, there was a confirmed capture of a specimen on Rannoch Moor in North Argyllshire in August 1969. Arran Browns are widespread in south-eastern and northern Europe.

Egg, caterpillar and chrysalis:

EGG (*page 211*): approx. 0·9 mm (w) × 1·2 mm (h); Almost spherical with smooth ribbing, shiny pale pinkish-brown, attached to a stalk.
CATERPILLAR (*page 218*): 35 mm; initially beige with narrow caramel-coloured stripes, becoming pinkish-grey with indistinct white stripes and with two tiny horns at its rear.
CHRYSALIS (*page 224*): approx. 17 mm; smooth and stubby; pinkish-brown with black markings and dots; formed on the ground.

Foodplants: a range of grasses including Red Fescue, and Wood Sedge.

190

Very similar to Scotch Argus but distinguished by the chequered fringes to both the upperside and underside of the wings.

M

F

F

Ad

Look for in late June to early August in woodland clearings above about 1,000 m.

Rannoch Moor at the summit of Glen Coe – possible Arran Brown habitat?

Species of doubtful provenance

There are many other butterfly species that have been recorded in the wild in the UK, although for a variety of reasons their occurrence is unlikely to be natural, and for some species the records are now considered doubtful:

- The ability of butterflies, especially the early life stages, to survive transportation, together with the natural range and migratory habits of the species in question all but rules out an unassisted occurrence.

- The ease by which many species can be bred in captivity, either by established butterfly houses or by private individuals, can lead to escapes and accidental or deliberate introductions. Given their range and habits, the possibility that some of these species have occurred naturally can be clearly ruled out. However, for other species, such as the extinct(?) Large Tortoiseshell (*page 184*) and potential colonists such as the Map (*page 178*), accidental or deliberate releases can cloud their true status in Britain and Ireland.

- In years gone by, some collectors were prone to the accidental or deliberate mis-labelling of specimens, diminishing the faith that current generations can have in some historical records.

A full list of the species recorded in Britain and Ireland can be found at **www.ukbutterflies.co.uk**, with photographs of the various life stages. This list includes species that are clearly of non-natural origin, but in a few cases the provenance of records is questionably natural. Although the species concerned most probably occurred through deliberate or accidental introductions, there is just a possibility that they could have occurred as genuine vagrants. Twelve of the species concerned are illustrated in this section, each with some explanatory notes.

Purple-shot Copper
Lycaena alciphron
Europe: four records, last in 1948 near Warwick – most likely accidentally imported as early life stage on animal fodder.

Sooty Copper *Lycaena tityrus*
Europe: four records, last in August 1958 in Sussex and August 1966 in Guernsey – non-migratory but possibly could be a wind-blown vagrant.

Moorland Clouded Yellow
Euchloe crameri
Europe and S Scandinavia: reported from the Sussex coast *ca.* 1820–1840 and one caught near Lewes in 1923 – not migratory but possibly associated with Clouded Yellow migration occurring at the time.

Cleopatra *Gonepteryx cleopatra*
S Europe and N Africa: approx. ten records, most recent in 1986 on Jersey and in 1981 in Kent – non-migratory, probably arrives via ship-assisted passage.

Mallow Skipper
Carcharodus alceae
Europe: two captured in Surrey in June 1923 – non-migratory so most likely an accidental import.

Oberthür's Grizzled Skipper
Pyrgus armoricanus
Europe: several captured in Norfolk in May/June *ca*. 1860 – probably accidentally imported as early stages on plants.

Green-underside Blue
Glaucopsyche alexis
W and N Europe: one captured in Torquay in September 1936 – non-migratory and very rare in September on the continent but possibly wind-blown.

Western Dappled White *Euchloe crameri*
Europe: four records, last in 1948 near Warwick – most likely accidentally imported as early life stage on animal fodder.

Spotted Fritillary *Melitaea didyma*
S and E Europe: four or five seen in Essex in August 1986 – probably a second brood from pregnant female that arrived on board a vessel.

False Grayling
Arethusana arethusa
Europe: one record, August 1974 near Ash Vale, Surrey – possibly a genuine immigrant, occurring at a time when other scarce migrant species were recorded, but most likely accidentally imported.

Large Wall *Lasiommata maera*
W Europe and Scandinavia: several records – probably accidentally introduced but possibly a genuine vagrant.

Woodland Grayling
Hipparchia fagi
Europe: one record, July 1946 near Oxted, Surrey – most likely accidentally imported.

Caterpillar foodplants

Butterflies are very particular about the foodplants they choose for their caterpillars and each species has its own preferences, with some caterpillars thriving only on one or just a few species. For example, the only known foodplant of the Small Blue is Kidney Vetch, and the butterfly's distribution is therefore restricted to areas where this plant grows. Other species are not so fussy, but still lay their eggs on only a limited range of plants. The Grizzled Skipper is usually associated with Wild Strawberry, but it will also lay on Agrimony and Creeping Cinquefoil and, occasionally, on several other plants.

The images that are included in this section are intended to lillustrate the common caterpillar foodplants of British and Irish butterflies, but be aware that caterpillars may not always be present when the plant is in flower. There are over 150 different plants that are used, although many only occasionally or if the preferred foodplants are unavailable. Those shown here are the plants, trees and grasses that are normally used – and where, by careful searching at the right time of year, caterpillars may be found.

How adult butterflies identify their preferred foodplants is a mystery. Some species make a careful inspection before they start egg-laying on the plant itself; others just drop their eggs in the vicinity of preferred plants and the caterpillars then have to search for food when they hatch. However, whichever strategy is adopted, timing is of the essence as eggs have to be laid so that tender plants are available when they hatch. Although nature generally ensures that this is the case, the balance is easily upset and there are numerous examples of butterflies being lost from an area because their habitat has been disrupted or destroyed by human activity.

NETTLES and HOP

Nettles and Hop are used as a foodplant by six species, and are favoured by some of our commonest butterflies.

Common Nettle
Small Tortoiseshell*, Red Admiral, Peacock, Comma, Painted Lady, Map*
* also **Small Nettle**

Hop
Red Admiral, Peacock, Comma

VETCHES and other legumes

Vetches are low-growing flowering plants related to peas, beans and lentils. They are found in a wide range of habitats and are popular caterpillar foodplants. The caterpillars of 15 butterfly species have been recorded feeding on vetches and other legumes.

Narrow-leaved Everlasting-pea
Long-tailed Blue*

* also **Broad-leaved Everlasting-pea** and **Bladder-senna**

Kidney Vetch
Small Blue

Meadow Vetchling
Wood White,
Cryptic Wood White

Lucerne
Clouded Yellow, Pale Clouded Yellow, Short-tailed Blue

Horseshoe Vetch
Chalkhill Blue, Silver-studded Blue, Adonis Blue, Berger's Clouded Yellow

Tufted Vetch
Wood White*, Cryptic Wood White*° Short-tailed Blue

* also **Bitter Vetch**
° also **Bush Vetch**

Clovers (Red Clover shown)
Clouded Yellow, Pale Clouded Yellow, Mazarine Blue, Short-tailed Blue

Common Bird's-foot-trefoil
Dingy Skipper*, Common Blue*, Silver-studded Blue, Green Hairstreak, Wood White*, Cryptic Wood White*, Short-tailed Blue

* also **Greater Bird's-foot-trefoil**

VIOLETS and PANSIES

Gardeners are familiar with these common pot plants, the result of cross-breeding from the wild species. Worldwide there are over 500 different wild violets and pansies, with colours ranging from violet through blue and yellow to white. These are the favoured caterpillar foodplants of six of the fritillaries.

Field Pansy
Queen of Spain Fritillary

Common Dog-violet – The Fritillary's choice
Pearl-bordered, Small Pearl-bordered*°, Dark Green*°, High Brown and Silver-washed Fritillaries
*also **Marsh Violet**   °also **Hairy Violet**

CRUCIFERS and WILD MIGNONETTE

Cultivated crucifers include cabbage, cauliflower, cress and other green-leaf vegetables. They all have flowers with four petals, arranged like a cross. In the wild, there are many early-flowering weeds such as Garlic Mustard, Charlock and Cuckooflower, which are often found growing along the margins of hedges. Wild Mignonette is not a crucifer but is often found on waste sites where it is easily seen with its high flowering spikes of six-petalled greenish-yellow flowers. Between them, the crucifers and Wild Mignonette support five butterfly species.

Hedge Mustard
Green-veined White, Orange-tip, Small White, Bath White

Charlock
Orange-tip, Small White, Green-veined White

Wild Mignonette
Small White, Large White, Bath White

Garlic Mustard
Orange-tip, Green-veined White

Cuckooflower
Orange-tip, Green-veined White*
* also **Wild Radish**

Water-cress
Green-veined White
+ **Large Bitter-cress**

Nasturtium
Small White*, Large White*, Green-veined White
* also cultivated *Brassica*

SHRUBS, TREES and CLIMBERS

There are many trees and shrubs that provide food for caterpillars. Two of the hairstreak species feed exclusively on Blackthorn and another feeds on elm foliage. White Admirals feed exclusively on Honeysuckle, and the elusive Purple Emperor on willows (Goat Willow and other species). In all, the caterpillars of 16 butterfly species feed on this type of plant

Honeysuckle
White Admiral

Blackthorn
Black Hairstreak, Brown Hairstreak, Black-veined White*
* also **Hawthorn**

Oaks
Purple Hairstreak
predominantly **Sessile Oak** and **Pendunculate Oak** (shown)

Willows (sallows)
Purple Emperor* (**Goat Willow** mainly), Camberwell Beauty, Comma (sometimes), Large Tortoiseshell, Scarce Tortoiseshell
* also **Crack-willow** and **Grey Willow**

Holly (left) and **Ivy** (right)
Holly Blue – spring brood uses Holly, summer brood uses Ivy

Alder Buckthorn
Brimstone
+ **Buckthorn**

English Elm
White-letter Hairstreak*, Camberwell Beauty, Large Tortoiseshell
* also **Wych** and **Small-leaved Elms**

Bilberry
Green Hairstreak

Gorse
Green Hairstreak, Silver-studded Blue

Broom
Green Hairstreak*, Long-tailed Blue
* also **Dyer's Greenweed**

OTHER PLANTS

There is a wide range of other flowering plants that find favour with butterfly caterpillars. Although eggs may be laid on or close to a developing bud, before leaves and flowers have formed, generally caterpillars eat steadily through tender new leaves. Some species eat alone, or at night, and some are accompanied by ants. Others munch communally during daylight within a silken web structure that they have spun around themselves and may be clearly visible, sometimes openly basking in sunshine on the outside of their web

Milk-parsley
Swallowtail

Dove's-foot Crane's-bill
Brown Argus

Wild Thyme
Large Blue

Potentillas – **Silverweed** (shown)
Tormentil, Creeping Cinquefoil
Grizzled Skipper

Wild Strawberry
Grizzled Skipper

Agrimony
Grizzled Skipper

Cross-leaved Heath, other heathers (Bell Heather shown)
Silver-studded Blue,
Green Hairstreak

Thistles (Creeping Thistle shown)
Painted Lady

Devil's-bit Scabious
Marsh Fritillary

Ribwort Plantain
Glanville Fritillary, Heath
Fritillary (DEVON AND CORNWALL)

Common Cow-wheat
Heath Fritillary

Foxglove
Heath Fritillary
(EXMOOR)

Germander Speedwell
Heath Fritillary
(DEVON AND CORNWALL)

Common Sorrel and
Sheep's Sorrel (shown)
Small Copper

Primrose
Duke of Burgundy

Cowslip
Duke of Burgundy

Common Rock-rose
Green Hairstreak, Brown Argus,
Northern Brown Argus,
Silver-studded Blue

199

Creeping Soft-grass
Small Skipper, Essex Skipper

Yorkshire-fog
Marbled White, Speckled Wood, Wall, Small Skipper

Common Couch
Ringlet, Speckled Wood, Gatekeeper, Essex Skipper

Timothy
Small Skipper, Essex Skipper

Cock's-foot
Meadow Brown, Ringlet, Speckled Wood, Wall, Large Skipper, Essex Skipper, Small Skipper

Tor Grass
Marbled White, Wall, Lulworth Skipper, Large Skipper, Essex Skipper

Hair-grasses –
Tufted Hair-grass
Ringlet, Grayling
Wavy Hair-grass
Wall
Early Hair-grass
Grayling

False Brome
Meadow Brown, Ringlet, Speckled Wood, Wall, Large Skipper, Small Skipper, Essex Skipper, Chequered Skipper (ENGLAND)

GRASSES

Many butterfly species use different grasses for their foodplants – which can be the most difficult plants to identify without a good deal of practice. In total, 18 species are associated with grasses, all of which are either browns or skippers.

Red Fescue
Marbled White,
Grayling, Arran Brown*

* also **Wood Sedge**

Sheep's-fescue
Marbled White,
Small Heath, Grayling,
Silver-spotted Skipper

Downy Oat-grass
Meadow Brown,
skippers

Common Bent
Meadow Brown,
Gatekeeper, Small
Heath, Wall

Purple Moor-grass
Chequered Skipper
(SCOTLAND), Scotch
Argus (SCOTLAND),
Large Skipper

Blue Moor-grass
Scotch Argus (ENGLAND)

Bristle Bent
Grayling

**Rough-stalked
Meadow-grass**
Meadow Brown,
Ringlet, Gatekeeper,
Small Heath

Mat-grass
Mountain Ringlet

Common Cottongrass
Large Heath

+ **Hare's-tail Cottongrass**

201

Butterfly nectar sources and caterpillar foodplants

The requirements of adult butterflies are usually vastly different from those of the caterpillar. Adults require nectar-rich plants in flower, and caterpillars require succulent vegetative matter. Whilst adults of many species are cosmopolitan in their choice of food sources, some are not; caterpillars tend to be very specific in their requirements.

This table shows what are recognized as the most important sources of food for both adults and caterpillars. **Bold text** indicates that the food source is one upon which the species is wholly or very largely dependent. *Italicized black text* is used to highlight those adult nectar sources that are non-specific. Green text is used to highlight any additional information of importance that is unrelated to the food sources. The species are listed in alphabetical order for ease of reference.

Species	Adult nectar source(s)	Caterpillar foodplant(s)	Page
Adonis Blue	Bramble, eyebrights, Horseshoe Vetch, Wild Marjoram, knapweeds, scabiouses, thistles	**Horsehoe Vetch.** *Attended by the ants Lasius alienus or Myrmica sabuleti*	98
Arran Brown	*Upland bog plants*	Tussock-forming grasses, Red Fescue; also White Sedge, other sedges and wood-rushes	190
Bath White	*Wide variety*	Crucifers, Wild Mignonette	164
Berger's Clouded Yellow	*Wide variety*	**Horsehoe Vetch**	166
Black Hairstreak	**Aphid honeydew,** Blackthorn, Wild Privet	**Blackthorn,** Wild Plum	80
Black-veined White	*Wide variety*	Blackthorn, Hawthorn	162
Brimstone	*Purple and mauve flowers*	Buckthorn, Alder Buckthorn	60
Brown Argus	Common Rock-rose; *wide variety of downland plants*	**Common Rock-rose,** Common Stork's-bill, Dove's-foot Crane's-bill. Often attended by the ants *Lasius alienus or Myrmica sabuleti*	90
Brown Hairstreak	**Aphid honeydew,** Common Fleabane, thistles, Bramble	**Blackthorn,** Bullace	78
Camberwell Beauty	*Wide variety*	Elms, poplars, willows	186
Chalkhill Blue	*Wide variety of chalk downland plants*	**Horsehoe Vetch**	100
Chequered Skipper	Bluebell, Bugle, Marsh Thistle	Purple Moor-grass (Scotland), [False Brome (England)]	52
Clouded Yellow	*Wide variety*	Clovers, Lucerne, Common Bird's-foot-trefoil	58
Comma	*Wide variety*	**Common Nettle,** Currants, elms, Hop, willows	136

Species	Adult nectar source(s)	Caterpillar foodplant(s)	Page
Common Blue	*Wide variety*	**Common** and Greater **Bird's-foot-trefoil**s, White Clover, *etc.* Attended by the ants *Formica rufa, Myrmica sabuleti*	96
Cryptic Wood White	*Wide variety*	**Meadow Vetchling**, Bush Vetch, Common Bird's-foot-trefoil, Greater Bird's-foot-trefoil, *etc.*	72
Dark Green Fritillary	Knapweeds, Red Clover, thistles; *purple and mauve flowers*	Hairy Violet, Marsh Violet, Common Dog-violet	120
Dingy Skipper	*Various but especially* Common Bird's-foot-trefoil	**Common Bird's-foot-trefoil**, Greater Bird's-foot-trefoil, Horseshoe Vetch	56
Duke of Burgundy	*Chalk downland plants in flower*	Cowslip, Primrose, False Oxlip	106
Essex Skipper	Field Scabious, Red Clover, thistles	**Cock's-foot**, Common Couch, Creeping Soft-grass, Timothy, *etc.*	44
Gatekeeper	Bramble, Common Fleabane, ragworts	Bents, fescues, Common Couch, meadow-grasses	146
Geranium Bronze	*Wide variety*	Cultivated *Pelargoniums*	176
Glanville Fritillary	Thrift; *assorted yellow flowers*	**Ribwort Plantain**	112
Grayling	*Heathland plants in flower*	Bristle Bent, Early Hair-grass, fescues, Marram, Tufted Hair-grass	144
Green Hairstreak	Hawkweeds, hawthorns	Common Rock-rose, Common Bird's-foot-trefoil, Broom, Gorse, Dogwood, Bilberry, *etc.*	76
Green-veined White	*Wide variety*	Charlock, Cuckooflower, Garlic Mustard, Water-cress, Hedge Mustard, Wild Cabbage, *etc.*	66
Grizzled Skipper	Common Bird's-foot-trefoil, buttercups, composites	**Wild Strawberry**, Silverweed, Tormentil, Creeping Cinquefoil, Agrimony, Dog-rose, *etc.*	54
Heath Fritillary	Bramble	**Common Cow-wheat**, Foxglove (Exmoor), Ribwort Plantain and Germander Speedwell (Devon and Cornwall)	108
High Brown Fritillary	Bramble, thistles	**Common Dog-violet, Hairy Violet**, Heath & Pale Dog-violets	118
Holly Blue	Bramble, forget-me-nots, Holly	**Holly** (spring), **Ivy** (summer); also Bramble, Spindle, *etc.*	86
Large Blue	*Chalk downland plants in flower*	**Wild Thyme**, Wild Marjoram, Later in nests of the ant *Myrmica sabuleti*	102
Large Copper	*Wide variety*	**Water Dock**	168

Species	Adult nectar source(s)	Caterpillar foodplant(s)	Page
Large Heath	Cross-leaved Heath; *blanket bog plants in flower*	**Hare's-tail Cottongrass**, other cottongrasses, Jointed Rush	158
Large Skipper	Bramble, thistles	**Cock's-foot**, False Brome, other grasses	50
Large Tortoiseshell	Willows (Spring), *wide variety* (Summer)	**Elms**, willows, poplars, birches	184
Large White	*Wide variety*	**Brassicas**, **crucifers**, Wild Mignonette, Nasturtium	62
Long-tailed Blue	*Wide variety*	Bladder-senna, everlasting-peas, Broom	170
Lulworth Skipper	Ragworts, Bramble, Wild Marjoram, Restharrow, thistles	**Tor-grass**	46
Map	*Wide variety*	Common Nettle, Small Nettle	178
Marbled White	Knapweeds, scabiouses, thistles	Red Fescue, Sheep's-fescue, Yorkshire-fog, Tor-grass	138
Marsh Fritillary	Betony, buttercups, Tormentil, Marsh Thistle	**Devil's-bit Scabious**, Small Scabious	110
Mazarine Blue	*Wide variety*	**Red Clover**	174
Meadow Brown	Thistles, *wide variety*	Bents, meadow-grasses, fescues, Cock's-foot, False Brome, Downy Oat-grass	148
Monarch	*Wide variety*	Milkweeds	188
Mountain Ringlet	Tormentil, *moorland plants in flower*	**Mat-grass** (and possibly other grasses)	152
Northern Brown Argus	*Limestone plants in flower*	**Common Rock-rose**	92
Orange-tip	Bugle, *crucifers*	Cuckooflower, Garlic Mustard, Charlock, many other crucifers	68
Painted Lady	*Wide variety*	**Thistles**, Common Nettle, Viper's-bugloss, mallows	130
Pale Clouded Yellow	*Wide variety*	Clovers, Lucerne	166
Peacock	Buddleias, Hemp-agrimony, teasels; *wide variety*	**Common Nettle**, Small Nettle, Hop	134
Pearl-bordered Fritillary	Bluebell, Bugle; *wide variety*	**Common Dog-violet**, Marsh Violet, other violets	116
Purple Emperor	**Aphid honeydew on oaks**	**Goat Willow**, Common (Grey) Willow	126
Purple Hairstreak	**Aphid honeydew on oaks**	**Oaks**	84
Queen of Spain Fritillary	*Wide variety*	Field Pansy, Wild Pansy	180
Red Admiral	*Wide variety*	**Common Nettle**, Small Nettle, Pellitory-of-the-wall, Hop	128

Species	Adult nectar source(s)	Caterpillar foodplant(s)	Page
Ringlet	Bramble, composites	*Variety of coarse grasses, e.g.* Cock's-foot, Common Couch, False Brome, Tufted Hair-grass, meadow-grasses	*150*
Scarce Tortoiseshell	*Wide variety*; flowering willows (Spring)	Willows; poplars	*182*
Scotch Argus	*Upland bog plants in flower*	Purple Moor-grass (Scotland); Blue Moor-grass (England)	*154*
Short-tailed Blue	*Wide variety*	Common Bird's-foot-trefoil, Red Clover, Tufted Vetch, Lucerne, legumes	*172*
Silver-spotted Skipper	Field Scabious, Red Clover, thistles	**Sheep's-fescue**	*48*
Silver-studded Blue	*Heathland plants in flower*	Common Bird's-foot-trefoil, vetches, heathers, heaths, Common Rock-rose. Attended by the ant *Lasius alienus*	*94*
Silver-washed Fritillary	Honeydew, Bramble, thistles	**Common Dog-violet**, Marsh Violet	*122*
Small Blue	Common Bird's-foot-trefoil, Kidney & Horseshoe Vetches	**Kidney Vetch**	*88*
Small Copper	Composites	Common Sorrel, Sheep's Sorrel, Kidney Vetch, Broad-leaved Dock	*104*
Small Heath	*Wide variety*	Bents, fescues – especially Sheep's-fescue, meadow-grasses	*156*
Small Pearl-bordered Fritillary	Common Bird's-foot-trefoil, Bluebell, Ragged-Robin	Common Dog-violet, Marsh Violet	*114*
Small Skipper	Field Scabious, Red Clover, thistles	Yorkshire-fog, Creeping Soft-grass, Timothy and other grasses	*42*
Small Tortoiseshell	*Wide variety*	**Common Nettle**, Small Nettle	*132*
Small White	*Wide variety*	Brassicas, crucifers, Nasturtium, Charlock, Wild Mignonette	*64*
Speckled Wood	**Aphid honeydew on Ash, birches, oaks**; ragworts	Cock's-foot, False Brome, Yorkshire-fog, Common Couch	*140*
Swallowtail	Milk-parsley	**Milk-parsley**	*74*
Wall	*Wide variety*	Cock's-foot, Tor-grass, Wavy Hair-grass, Yorkshire-fog, False Brome and other grasses	*142*
White Admiral	Aphid honeydew on oaks, Bramble	**Honeysuckle**	*124*
White-letter Hairstreak	**Aphid honeydew on elms**, Bramble, Creeping Thistle	English Elm, Small-leaved Elm, Wych Elm	*82*
Wood White	*Woodland plants in flower*	Meadow Vetchling, Tufted Vetch, Common Bird's-foot-trefoil, Greater Bird's-foot-trefoil	*70*

Eggs, caterpillars and chrysalises

Depicted in this section are the early life stages of all of Britain and Ireland's resident and migrant breeding species, except for a few for which images are unavailable to the best of our knowledge.

Eggs are shown at 10× life-size, and the caterpillars and chrysalises at life-size. Approximate dimensions are given for each of the life stages. Caterpillar length is when fully grown, ready to pupate. All dimensions vary and the figures given are only intended to be a guide. There is a brief description of where and the time of year that eggs, caterpillars and chrysalises are most likely to be found. Blue text indicates that the species overwinters at this stage. *Italicized text indicates that the species is not currently known to breed in the wild in Britain or Ireland.* A fuller description and additional information on the early life stages can be found in the relevant species account on the page indicated.

Please be aware that it is not advisable to collect eggs, caterpillars or chrysalises in order to observe their development. Many species have very specific requirements in terms of the favoured species of foodplant, as well as its freshness, location and the part of the plant preferred. In addition, for a good number of species (see *page 232*) it is illegal to disturb any of the early life stages as well as the adults.

Glanville Fritillary (page 112) caterpillars venture to the top of their web to bask in sunshine.

A description of the egg can be found in the relevant species account

Small White *p. 64*
0·4 mm (w) × 1·0 mm (h)
Singly; on underside of leaf

May–June + August–Sep

Green-veined White *p. 66*
0·4 mm (w) × 1·0 mm (h)
Singly; on underside of leaf

May–June + August/Sep

Clouded Yellow *p. 58*
0·4 mm (w) × 1·1 mm (h)
Singly; on upperside of leaf

June + August–October

Brimstone *p. 60*
0·5 mm (w) × 1·3 mm (h)
Singly; on underside of
young leaves
End May–June

Pale Clouded Yellow *p. 166*
0·4 mm (w) × 1·0 mm (h)
Singly; on upperside of leaf

May–June + August–September

Orange-tip *p. 68*
0·6 mm (w) × 1·2 mm (h)
Singly; on flower-stalk

April–June

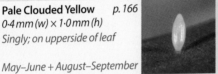

Berger's Clouded Yellow
p. 166
0·4 mm (w) × 1·0 mm (h)
Singly; on upperside of leaf
May–June + August–September

Bath White *p. 164*
0·4 mm (w) × 0·85 mm (h)
Singly; on foodplant

July

Wood White *p. 70*
0·5 mm (w) × 1·3 mm (h)
Singly; on underside of leaf

June–July

Cryptic Wood White *p. 72*
0·5 mm (w) × 1·3 mm (h)
Singly; on underside of leaf

May/June–July

Large White *p. 62*
0·6 mm (w) × 1·4 mm (h)
In clusters; on either side of leaf

May–June + August–September

Black-veined White *p. 162*
0·5 mm (w) × 1·0 mm (h)
In batches; on foodplant

July

EGGS (10 × life-size)

A description of the egg can be found in the relevant species account

Swallowtail *p. 74*
1·0 mm (w) × 0·9 mm (h)
Singly; on tall Milk-parsley plants
May/June + September

Monarch *p. 188*
0·8 mm (w) × 1·2 mm (h)
Singly; on leaf

June–October (unlikely)

Holly Blue *p. 86*
0·7 mm (w) × 0·4 mm (h)
Singly; at base of flower bud: Holly (spring); Ivy (summer)
May + early August

Small Blue *p. 88*
0·45 mm (w) × 0·2 mm (h)
Singly; within flower-head

June + late August

Brown Argus *p. 90*
0·5 mm (w) × 0·3 mm (h)
Singly; on underside of leaf

May/June + late July–Sep

Northern Brown Argus *p. 92*
0·6 mm (w) × 0·3 mm (h)
Singly; on upperside of leaf

July

Silver-studded Blue *p. 94*
0·6 mm (w) × 0·3 mm (h)
Singly; on foodplant or ground; near ants' nest
August–March

Common Blue *p. 96*
0·5 mm (w) × 0·2 mm (h)
Singly; on tiny, tender leaves

June + Aug/Sep + late Oct

Adonis Blue *p. 98*
0·5 mm (w) × 0·3 mm (h)
Singly; on underside of small Horseshoe Vetch leaf
June + September

Chalkhill Blue *p. 100*
0·5 mm (w) × 0·3 mm (h)
Singly; on or near Horseshoe Vetch
August– March

Large Blue *p. 102*
0·5 mm (w) × 0·3 mm (h)
Singly; in flower-heads

July

Mazarine Blue *p. 174*
0·55 mm (w) × 0·3 mm (h)
Singly; in flower-heads of foodplant
July

Long-tailed Blue *p. 170*
0·5 mm (w) × 0·3 mm (h)
Singly; on flower-heads of foodplant
July–August

Short-tailed Blue *p. 172*
0·45 mm (w) × 0·2 mm (h)
Singly; on flower-heads of foodplant
July–August

Duke of Burgundy *p. 106*
0·6 mm (w) × 0·6 mm (h)
Small groups; close to edge of underside of leaf
June

A description of the egg can be found in the relevant species account

Small Skipper *p. 42*
0·85 mm (w) × 0·5 mm (h)
In clusters on grass stem

June–August

Essex Skipper *p. 44*
0·8 mm (w) × 0·3 mm (h)
In clusters within grass sheath

August–March

Lulworth Skipper *p. 46*
1·6 mm (w) × 0·8 mm (h)
In rows within flower sheath

July–September

Silver-spotted Skipper *p. 48*
0·9 mm (w) × 0·7 mm (h)
Singly

August–March

Large Skipper *p. 50*
1·1 mm (w) × 0·8 mm (h)
Singly; on underside of grass blade
July–August

Chequered Skipper *p. 52*
0·6 mm (w) × 0·5 mm (h)
Singly; on underside of grass blade
June

Grizzled Skipper *p. 54*
0·6 mm (w) × 0·5 mm (h)
Singly; on underside of leaf

May–June

Dingy Skipper *p. 56*
0·5 mm (w) × 0·5 mm (h)
Singly; on underside of grass blade
June–July

Heath Fritillary *p. 108*
0·4 mm (w) × 0·5 mm (h)
Large batches; on underside of leaf
Mid-June–August

Marsh Fritillary *p. 110*
0·7 mm (w) × 0·8 mm (h)
Large batches; on underside of leaf
Mid-June–July

Glanville Fritillary *p. 112*
0·4 mm (w) × 0·5 mm (h)
Large batches; on underside of leaf
June

Small Pearl-bordered Fritillary *p. 114*
0·5 mm (w) × 0·65 mm (h)
Singly; on underside of leaf
June–July

Pearl-bordered Fritillary
p. 116
0·6 mm (w) × 0·8 mm (h)
Singly; on underside of leaf
June

High Brown Fritillary *p. 118*
0·6 mm (w) × 0·8 mm (h)
Singly; on twigs, leaves or stones
Mid-July–March

Dark Green Fritillary *p. 120*
0·8 mm (w) × 1·0 mm (h)
Singly; on foodplant or nearby
August–September

Silver-washed Fritillary *p. 122*
1·0 mm (w) × 1·0 mm (h)
Singly; in crevices on bark

August–September

EGGS (10× life-size)

A description of the egg can be found in the relevant species account

Small Copper　　　*p. 104*
0·6 mm (w) × 0·3 mm (h)
Usually singly; on underside
of leaf
June + August + October

Green Hairstreak　　　*p. 76*
0·3 mm (w) × 0·65 mm (w)
Singly; on tender shoot or
flower bud
June

Brown Hairstreak　　　*p. 78*
0·7 mm (w) × 0·6 mm (h)
Singly; on young twigs

September–April

Purple Hairstreak　　　*p. 84*
0·8 mm (w) × 0·5 mm (h)
Singly or in pairs; on tips of
branches
August–March

White-letter Hairstreak
　　　　　　　　　p. 82
0·8 mm (w) × 0·4 mm (h)
Singly; on twigs
August–March

Black Hairstreak　　　*p. 80*
0·8 mm (w) × 0·4 mm (h)
Singly; on mature twigs

July–April

White Admiral　　　*p. 124*
0·9 mm (w) × 0·9 mm (h)
Singly; close to edge of
upperside of leaf
July/August

Purple Emperor　　　*p. 126*
1·2 mm (w) × 1·0 mm (h)
Singly; on upperside of leaf

August

Red Admiral　　　*p. 128*
0·6 mm (w) × 0·8 mm (h)
Singly; on upperside of leaf

April–August

Painted Lady　　　*p. 130*
0·6 mm (w) × 0·65 mm (h)
Singly; on upperside of leaf

April–July + August–Oct

Small Tortoiseshell　　　*p. 132*
0·75 mm (w) × 0·85 mm (h)
In clusters; on underside of
leaf
May + July

Peacock　　　*p. 134*
0·7 mm (w) × 0·8 mm (h)
In clusters; on underside of
leaf
May

Comma　　　*p. 136*
0·65 mm (w) × 0·8 mm (h)
Singly; on upperside of leaf

April/May + July

Large Tortoiseshell　　　*p. 184*
0·6 mm (w) × 0·9 mm (h)
In batches around twigs

April–May

Map　　　*p. 178*
dimensions not recorded
In strings; on underside of leaf

May–June + July–August

A description of the egg can be found in the relevant species account

Marbled White *p. 138*
1·0 mm (w) × 1·0 mm (w)
Scattered on ground near foodplant
July–August

Speckled Wood *p. 140*
0·8 mm (w) × 0·8 mm (h)
Singly; on plants in sunlight (spring) or shade (summer)
April–June + July–October

Wall *p. 142*
0·9 mm (w) × 0·9 mm (h)
Singly, or in clusters
June + August–September + mid-October

Grayling *p. 144*
0·7 mm (w) × 0·8 mm (h)
Singly; on foodplant or nearby debris
July–September

Gatekeeper *p. 146*
0·65 mm (w) × 0·7 mm (h)
Singly; on grass or in long grass at the base of shrubs
July–August

Meadow Brown *p. 148*
0·5 mm (w) × 0·5 mm (h)
Singly; on grass blades

July–September

Ringlet *p. 150*
0·8 mm (w) × 0·9 mm (h)
Scattered amongst grass

July/August

Mountain Ringlet *p. 152*
0·8 mm (w) × 1·2 mm (h)
Singly; on blade of Mat-grass

July

Scotch Argus *p. 154*
1·0 mm (w) × 1·3 mm (h)
Singly; on grass blades or flowers
August

Small Heath *p. 156*
0·5 mm (w) × 0·7 mm (h)
Singly; on grass blades

June/July + August–October

Large Heath *p. 158*
0·8 mm (w) × 0·8 mm (h)
Singly; on foodplant, often at the base
July/August

Arran Brown *p. 190*
0·9 mm (w) × 1·2 mm (h)
Singly; on grass stalk

July–following May

A cluster of Small Tortoiseshell eggs on the underside of a Common Nettle leaf (left); A cluster of Large Tortoiseshell (presumed extinct in the UK) eggs wrapped around an elm twig (centre); and the distinctive strings of Map (yet to be proven to breed naturally in the UK) eggs (right).

CATERPILLARS (Fully-grown size)

A description of the caterpillar can be found in the relevant species account

Brimstone *p.60*
32–34mm
Rests on midrib and eats surrounding leaf

June–July

Orange-tip *p.68*
31mm
Mainly on seed pods of foodplant, sometimes on flowers and leaves
May–July

Green-veined White *p.66*
25mm
On leaves of foodplant

May–July + Aug–Sep

Small White *p.64*
25mm
Feeds in heart of plant when young; rests on leaf midrib

May–July + Aug–Sep

Wood White *p.70*
19mm
Rests on plant stems

June/July

Cryptic Wood White *p.72*
19mm
Probably not possible to differentiate from Wood White

June–July

Pale Clouded Yellow *p.166*
32mm
Conspicuous on foodplant; unable to survive British winter
June–July + [Sep/Oct]

Clouded Yellow *p.58*
33mm
Conspicuous on foodplant

June/July + Sep–Oct

Berger's Clouded Yellow *p.166*
32mm
Conspicuous on foodplant; unable to survive British winter
June–July + [Sep/Oct]

Bath White *p.164*
25mm
Conspicuous, feeding by day and by night

July–August

A description of the caterpillar can be found in the relevant species account

Large White *p. 62*
45 mm
Conspicuous on outer leaves of foodplant

May–July + Aug–Sep

Black-veined White *p. 162*
38 mm
Conspicuous, feeds in small groups

July–following June

Swallowtail *p. 74*
52mm
Exclusively on Milk-parsley; reminiscent of
bird-dropping when young (*inset*)

June–July + late September

Monarch *p. 188*
56 mm
Conspicuous; poisonous to predators

June–October (unlikely)

CATERPILLARS (Fully-grown size)

A description of the caterpillar can be found in the relevant species account

Small Skipper   *p. 42*
20–25 mm
Overwinters inside cocoon within grass sheath; feeds inside built grass 'tube', but outside when fully-grown
August–May

Essex Skipper   *p. 44*
20–24 mm
Within built grass 'tube'; moves outside 'tube' to feed
April–June

Lulworth Skipper   *p. 46*
25 mm
Overwinters inside cocoon within grass sheath; nocturnal feeder, stays within built grass 'tube' during the day
August–May

Silver-spotted Skipper   *p. 48*
25 mm
Feeds within a 'tent' formed by binding together grass blades
April–July

Large Skipper   *p. 50*
28 mm
Overwinters within built grass 'tube'; feeds on leaves above 'tube'
August–May

Chequered Skipper   *p. 52*
25 mm
Feeds within built grass 'tube'; hibernates in grass blades spun together with silk
July–April

Grizzled Skipper   *p. 54*
18 mm
Feeds early morning and evening from within spun silk tent
June–July

Dingy Skipper   *p. 56*
17 mm
Feeds within built grass 'tube'; hibernates in grass blades spun together with silk
July–April

Black Hairstreak   *p. 80*
16 mm
At first on flower buds, but on leaves when mature
May

Green Hairstreak   *p. 76*
16–18 mm
Feeds on young leaves
June–July

Brown Hairstreak   *p. 78*
18 mm
Nocturnal; rests by day on underside of leaf; purple before pupation   May–June

White-letter Hairstreak   *p. 82*
16 mm
At first on flower buds, but on leaves when mature
April–May

Purple Hairstreak   *p. 84*
16 mm
Nocturnal; rests by day under an oak bud
March–May

A description of the caterpillar can be found in the relevant species account

Duke of Burgundy *p. 106*
16 mm
Nocturnal; feeding on upperside of leaves
June/July

Small Copper *p. 104*
16 mm
On underside of leaf

June + August + Oct–March

Large Blue *p. 102*
15 mm
On flowers; on ant grubs within nest when mature/ overwintering   August–May

Holly Blue *p. 86*
15 mm
On flower buds

May–June + August/Sep

Brown Argus *p. 90*
11 mm
On underside of leaf when young; above when mature
June–July + Sep–April

Northern Brown Argus
12 mm   *p. 92*
On underside of leaf; hibernates at base of foodplant   July–May

Silver-studded Blue *p. 94*
13 mm
On flower buds and young shoots
April–May

Common Blue *p. 96*
13 mm
On underside of leaf; hibernates at foodplant base
June–July + August–April

Adonis Blue *p. 98*
15 mm
Feeds by day; rests at base of foodplant; overwinters in soil   June–July + Sep–April

Chalkhill Blue *p. 100*
16 mm
Nocturnal; by day hides at base of foodplant
April–June

Small Blue *p. 88*
9·5 mm
Feeds within flower-head; overwinters under moss or in soil   June–April

Mazarine Blue *p. 174*
10 mm
Young in flower heads; on shoots after hibernation
July–May

Short-tailed Blue *p. 172*
9–10 mm
Flowers and fresh shoots

August–September

Long-tailed Blue *p. 170*
15 mm
On flowers; continues to develop within a seed pod
August–September

CATERPILLARS (Fully-grown size)
A description of the caterpillar can be found in the relevant species account

Pearl-bordered Fritillary
p. 116
20–25 mm
Feeds on leaf-litter, will bask; overwinters in leaf
June–Aug + Aug–April

Small Pearl-bordered Fritillary
p. 114
21 mm
Feeds in shade; overwinters in leaf
June–Aug + Aug–May

Heath Fritillary
p. 108
22–25 mm
Young in communal web; individuals overwinter in curled-up leaf
July–April

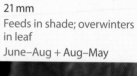

Queen of Spain Fritillary
32 mm
p. 180
Only active on warm days

June/July + [Sep–Nov]

Glanville Fritillary
p. 112
25 mm
Feeds/hibernates within communal web
July–April

Marsh Fritillary
p. 110
26–30 mm
Feeds/hibernates within communal web
July–April

High Brown Fritillary
p. 118
38 mm
Conspicuous on foodplant

March–May

Dark Green Fritillary
p. 120
35–40 mm
Overwinters in curled-up leaf; very active in spring
August–May

Silver-washed Fritillary
p. 122
38 mm
Overwinters in crevice; on violets in spring
August–May

Map
p. 178
20 mm
In Europe, two or sometimes three broods, feeding on nettles
May–June + July–August

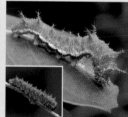

White Admiral
p. 124
25–29 mm
Overwinters in leaf 'tent'; rests along midrib when mature
August–May

young caterpillar

Red Admiral *p. 128*
35 mm
Feeds in a 'tent' formed from folded leaves
May–September

Small Tortoiseshell *p. 132*
32 mm
Gregarious within communal web
May/June + July–August

Painted Lady *p. 130*
30 mm
Feeds in a 'tent' formed from folded leaves
May–July + Sep–Oct

Comma *p. 136*
32–35 mm
Conspicuous on upperside of leaf
May + July/August

Peacock *p. 134*
42 mm
Gregarious within communal web
End May–June

Large Tortoiseshell *p. 184*
45 mm
Gregarious within communal web
May/June

young caterpillar

Scarce Tortoiseshell *p. 182*
40 mm
Live communally in conspicuous silken tents
May–June

Purple Emperor *p. 126*
35–40 mm
Overwinters adjacent to bud; cryptic against leaf
September–June

Camberwell Beauty *p. 186*
50 mm
In groups until dispersing before pupation
June–August

CATERPILLARS (Fully-grown size)

A description of the caterpillar can be found in the relevant species account

Marbled White p. 138
28 mm

Overwinters deep in grass tussock; feeds by night when mature; rests by day on grass stem

August–May

Speckled Wood p. 140
28 mm

On underside of leaf; some overwinter in base of foodplant

May–June + July–Sep + September–March

Wall p. 142
24 mm

Mainly nocturnal; on leaves; some overwinter in base of foodplant

June + Aug/Sep + Oct–April

Grayling p. 144
30 mm

Feeds by day when young; at base of grass tussock; nocturnal when mature, rests by day in grass tussock

August–June

Gatekeeper p. 146
25 mm

Feeds by day when young; overwinters in base of grass tussock; feeds by night when mature

August–June

Meadow Brown p. 148
25 mm

Feeds by day when young; overwinters hidden at base of grass tussock; feeds by night when mature

July–May

Ringlet p. 150
21 mm

Nocturnal; overwinters in base of grass tussock; rests by day in grass tussock

August–May

Mountain Ringlet p. 152
19–20 mm

Overwinters in grass tussocks; feeds on tender leaves

August–April

Scotch Argus p. 154
27 mm

Feeds by day when young; overwinters in leaf-litter; nocturnal when mature, rests by day on ground

September–June

Small Heath p. 156
20 mm

Nocturnal; by day hidden in base of grass tussock; overwinters deep in tussock

June–July + Sept–April

Arran Brown p. 190
35 mm

Feeds on a variety of grasses; two-year cycle

April–the following year

Large Heath p. 158
25 mm

On tender leaves; hidden in tussock when not feeding; overwinters deep in tussock

August–May

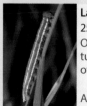

A description of the chrysalis can be found in the relevant species account

Brimstone   p. 60
22–24 mm
Usually away from foodplant; attached to stem or underside of leaf
End July–early August

Clouded Yellow   p. 58
22 mm
On stem of foodplant

July + Oct

Pale Clouded Yellow   p. 166
22 mm
Upright; attached to stem with silk thread

June–July + [Sep/Oct]

Berger's Clouded Yellow   p. 166
22 mm
Upright; attached to stem with silk thread

June–July + [Sep/Oct]

Large White   p. 62
20 mm
Often found away from foodplant, even found on fences, trees etc
June/July + Sep–April

Small White   p. 64
19 mm
Often found away from foodplant, even found on fences, trees etc
June/July + Sep–April

Green-veined White   p. 66
19 mm
Away from foodplant, low down in vegetation
June/July + Sep–April

Orange-tip   p. 68
23 mm
Upright; attached to stem with silk thread; overwinters

July–May

Wood White   p. 70
16 mm
Upright; attached to stem with silk thread; some overwinter

July–May

Cryptic Wood White   p. 72
16 mm
For possible minor differences from Wood White, see species text
August–May

Bath White   p. 164
19 mm
On stem of foodplant, or nearby

probably August

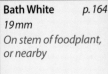
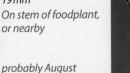

Black-veined White   p. 162
25 mm
Attached to stem of foodplant

May–July

CHRYSALISES (Life-size)

A description of the chrysalis can be found in the relevant species account

Small Skipper   *p. 42*
16–20 mm

At base of foodplant; within leaf 'tent' bound by silk threads

June

Essex Skipper   *p. 44*
15–17 mm

At base of foodplant; within leaf 'tent' bound by silk threads

End June–July

Lulworth Skipper   *p. 46*
17 mm

At base of foodplant; within leaf 'tent' bound by silk threads

May–July

Silver-spotted Skipper   *p. 48*
15 mm

Within spun cocoon in grass tussock

End July–early August

Large Skipper   *p. 50*
19 mm

Hidden in grass tussock; within loose cocoon

End May–mid-June

Chequered Skipper   *p. 52*
16 mm

Hidden amongst dead grass leaves that have been bound together

April–mid-May

Grizzled Skipper   *p. 54*
13 mm

Overwinters at base of foodplant; within silk 'tent'

July–April

Dingy Skipper   *p. 56*
14 mm

Within leaf 'tent' bound by silk thread

May + mid-August

Duke of Burgundy   *p. 106*
9 mm

Overwinters; in leaf-litter or grass tussock
August–May

Green Hairstreak   *p. 76*
8–9.5 mm

Overwinters; underground, possibly in ants' nest
August–May

Brown Hairstreak   *p. 78*
12 mm

On ground in crevice, at base of grass or in leaf-litter
End June–July

White-letter Hairstreak   *p. 82*
9 mm

Attached to stem or leaf

June/July

Black Hairstreak   *p. 80*
9.5 mm

Attached to twig or leaf

June

Purple Hairstreak   *p. 84*
10 mm

In loose cocoon; beneath soil, sometimes in ants' nest
June/July

A description of the chrysalis can be found in the relevant species account

Holly Blue *p. 86*
8–9mm
On or near ground;
well hidden
July + September–April

Small Blue *p. 88*
8mm
Attached to Kidney Vetch

April/May + mid-August

Brown Argus *p. 90*
8mm
On ground at base of
foodplant
April/May + July/August

Northern Brown Argus
8·5mm *p. 92*
In loose vegetation near
foodplant
May/June

Silver-studded Blue *p. 94*
8–9mm
Underground or in ants' nest

June

Common Blue *p. 96*
9–10mm
On ground or base of
foodplant
April–May + July–August

Adonis Blue *p. 98*
11mm
On ground or in ants' nest

May + August

Chalkhill Blue *p. 100*
12mm
On ground at base of
foodplant; buried by ants
June–July

Large Blue *p. 102*
13mm
Formed in ants' nest

May/June

Small Copper *p. 104*
10·5mm
On ground amongst leaf-
litter
April + early July + Sep

Short-tailed Blue *p. 172*
8mm
On or close to foodplant

July–September

Long-tailed Blue *p. 170*
12mm
Close to foodplant

August–September

Mazarine Blue *p. 174*
10mm
Close to foodplant

May–June

221

CHRYSALISES (Life-size)

A description of the chrysalis can be found in the relevant species account

Pearl-bordered Fritillary *p. 116*

14 mm

Low down in vegetation

May + mid-August

Small Pearl-bordered Fritillary *p. 114*

15 mm

Low down in leaf-litter

May/June + mid-August

Heath Fritillary *p. 108*

12·5 mm

Attached upside-down to dead vegetation

May–June + mid-August

Marsh Fritillary *p. 110*

12–15 mm

Hangs upside-down attached to leaf or stem

April/May

High Brown Fritillary *p. 118*

20 mm

Hangs upside-down within loose silk 'tent'

June/July

Dark Green Fritillary *p. 120*

20 mm

Upside-down within loose 'tent' of leaves

June/July

Silver-washed Fritillary *p. 122*

22 mm

Hangs upside-down attached to leaf or twig

June

Queen of Spain Fritillary *p. 180*

17–19 mm

Hangs upside-down attached to leaf or stem

July + September/October

Glanville Fritillary *p. 112*

13–15 mm

In loose silk 'tent' in rock crevice or vegetation

April/May + July/August

Map *p. 178*

dimensions not recorded

Hangs upside-down from a stem or twig

June–July + September–May

Red Admiral — p. 128
22–24 mm
Within 'tent' formed from folded leaves
July–October

Small Tortoiseshell — p. 132
20–22 mm
Hangs upside-down attached to leaf or stem
June + August/September

Comma — p. 136
21 mm
Hangs upside-down attached to leaf or stem
June + August

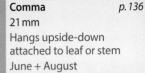
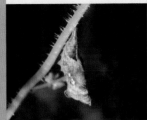

Painted Lady — p. 130
25 mm
Within 'tent' formed from folded leaves
June–October

Peacock — p. 134
25–29 mm
Hangs upside-down attached to leaf or stem
July

Large Tortoiseshell — p. 184
27 mm
Hangs upside-down attached to twig or stem
June

Camberwell Beauty — p. 186
25–32 mm
Hangs upside-down from a stem or twig
July–August

White Admiral — p. 124
22 mm
Hangs upside-down attached to leaf or stem
June

Purple Emperor — p. 126
30–35 mm
Hangs upside-down attached to leaf or stem
June/July

CHRYSALISES (Life-size)

A description of the chrysalis can be found in the relevant species account

Marbled White p.138 12–15mm Loose on the ground under soil or moss June–mid-July	**Speckled Wood** p.140 18mm Attached to grass stem Late May–Aug + Sep–April
Wall p.142 16mm Attached to foodplant or nearby vegetation April/May + July + end Sep	**Grayling** p.144 16mm Below ground in a hollow lined with silk Mid-June–August
Gatekeeper p.146 12mm Low down in vegetation; usually hidden under a leaf Mid-June–August	**Meadow Brown** p.148 16mm Low down in vegetation May–August
Ringlet p.150 11–13mm In loose cocoon; in moss at the base of grass tussock June/July	**Mountain Ringlet** p.152 10–11mm In loose cocoon; hidden deep in Mat-grass tussock May–June
Scotch Argus p.154 13mm In loose cocoon; hidden at the base of grass tussock Mid-June–July	**Small Heath** p.156 8·5mm Attached to grass stem April–May + July–Sep
Arran Brown p.190 *17mm* *On the ground near its foodplant* *May–June*	**Large Heath** p.158 11mm Attached to foodplant or nearby vegetation Late May–mid-July

Swallowtail p.74
28–32mm
Attached upright to woody stem near to foodplant

July–May

Monarch p.188
22mm
Hanging from a leaf or stalk

June–October (unlikely)

List of British and Irish Butterflies

The following list provides a summary of the status of the 81 species that are, or have been, resident or occurred as a migrant to Britain or Ireland, including six that have been recorded so rarely that their occurence is regarded as accidental (vagrants), and those species that have been introduced as part of a licensed conservation programme, or have been accidentally introduced and subsequently bred.

The species are listed in taxonomic order and the entries in the Status/notes column are colour-coded as follows:

Resident species that is of little or no conservation concern	Green tint
Resident species that is of particular conservation concern	Red tint
Annual (dark blue), irregular (mid-blue) or rare (pale blue) migrant species/races	Blue tint
Reintroduced (dark purple) and accidentally introduced (pale purple) species	Purple tint
Former breeding species/race that is now extinct in Britain	Red tint/red text

English name	Scientific name	Status/notes	Page
Family: HESPERIIDAE – Subfamily: Heteropterinae			
Chequered Skipper	*Carterocephalus palaemon*	Localized resident	52
Large Chequered Skipper	*Heteropterus morpheus*	Accidental introduction Jersey: discovered in 1946 probably on hay imported from France during the Second World War; no sightings since 1996.	160
Family: HESPERIIDAE – Subfamily: Hesperiinae			
Small Skipper	*Thymelicus sylvestris*	Common resident	42
Essex Skipper	*Thymelicus lineola*	Common resident	44
Lulworth Skipper	*Thymelicus acteon*	Localized resident	46
Silver-spotted Skipper	*Hesperia comma*	Localized resident	48
Large Skipper	*Ochlodes sylvanus*	Common resident	50
Family: HESPERIIDAE – Subfamily: Pyrginae			
Dingy Skipper	*Erynnis tages*	Localized resident race *tages*: throughout Britain and Ireland, except W Ireland race *baynesi*: W Ireland (The Burren and SE Galway)	56
Grizzled Skipper	*Pyrgus malvae*	Declining resident	54

English name	Scientific name	Status/notes	Page
Family: PAPILIONIDAE – Subfamily: Parnassiinae			
Apollo	*Parnassius apollo*	Probable vagrant (last record 1986) from Europe and Scandinavia; mainly recorded from SE England but also Scotland – some/all records may be from accidental imports or deliberate releases but has occurred in years of large-scale immigrations of other spp.	*160*
Family: PAPILIONIDAE – Subfamily: Papilioninae			
Swallowtail	*Papilio machaon*	Localized resident race *britannicus*: endemic to Britain Rare migrant race *gorganus*: from continental Europe	*74*
Scarce Swallowtail	*Iphiclides podalirius*	Probable vagrant (20+ records; last in 2003) from N Africa and S Europe. Some/all may be from accidental imports or deliberate releases, though there is the slight possibility that some records may relate to genuine vagrancy.	*160*
Family: PIERIDAE – Subfamily: Dismorphinae			
Wood White	*Leptidea sinapis*	Rare resident race *sinapis*: Britain and most of Ireland race *juvernica*: W Ireland (The Burren, SE Galway, Clare)	*70*
Cryptic Wood White	*Leptidea juvernica*	Rare resident (Ireland only)	*72*
Family: PIERIDAE – Subfamily: Coliadinae			
Pale Clouded Yellow	*Colias hyale*	Rare migrant from N France/central Europe	*166*
Berger's Clouded Yellow	*Colias alfacariensis*	Rare migrant from central and S Europe	*166*
Clouded Yellow	*Colias croceus*	Annual migrant/breeder from N Africa/S Europe	*58*
Brimstone	*Gonepteryx rhamni*	Widespread resident race *rhamni*: Britain race *gravesi*: Ireland	*60*
Family: PIERIDAE – Subfamily: Pierinae			
Black-veined White	*Aporia crataegi*	Extinct *ca.* 1925	*162*
Large White	*Pieris brassicae*	Common resident	*62*
Small White	*Pieris rapae*	Abundant resident	*64*
Green-veined White	*Pieris napi*	Common resident race *sabellicae*: England and Wales race *thomsoni*: Scotland race *britannica*: Ireland	*66*
Bath White	*Pontis daplidice*	Rare migrant from S Europe	*164*
Orange-tip	*Anthocharis cardamines*	Widespread resident race *britannica*: Britain race *hibernica*: Ireland	*68*

English name	Scientific name	Status/notes	Page
Family: LYCAENIDAE – Subfamily: Theclinae			
Green Hairstreak	*Callophrys rubi*	Widespread resident	76
Brown Hairstreak	*Thecla betulae*	Localized resident	78
Purple Hairstreak	*Neozephyrus quercus*	Widespread resident	84
White-letter Hairstreak	*Satyrium w-album*	Widespread resident	82
Black Hairstreak	*Satyrium pruni*	Rare resident	80
Family: LYCAENIDAE – Subfamily: Lycaeninae			
Small Copper	*Lycaena phlaeas*	Common resident race *eleus*: Britain race *hibernica*: Ireland	104
Large Copper	*Lycaena dispar*	Extinct *ca.*1850 (race *dispar*) Attempted reintroductions of races *rutilus* (from Germany in 1909) and *batavus* (from Holland in 1930) failed.	168
Family: LYCAENIDAE – Subfamily: Polyommatinae			
Long-tailed Blue	*Lampides boeticus*	Rare migrant from continental Europe	170
Geranium Bronze	*Cacyreus marshalli*	Accidental introduction Introduced to Europe from South Africa on imported *Pelargoniums*	176
Lang's Short-tailed Blue	*Leptotes pirithous*	Vagrant (one record: 1938) N Africa/S Europe	160
Small Blue	*Cupido minimus*	Declining resident	88
Short-tailed Blue	*Cupido argiades*	Vagrant (<20 records) from continental Europe	172
Silver-studded Blue	*Plebeius argus*	Localized resident race *argus*: throughout range race *caernensis*: Great Orme, Conwy race *cretaceus* (probably extinct *ca.*1942): formerly Portland Bill, Dorset (?); Kent; Surrey and Essex race *masseyi* (extinct *ca.*1975): formerly Lancashire and S Cumbria	94
Brown Argus	*Aricia agestis*	Widespread resident	90
Northern Brown Argus	*Aricia artaxerxes*	Localized resident race *artaxerxes*: Scotland race *salmacis*: N England	92
Common Blue	*Polyommatus icarus*	Widespread resident race *icarus*: Britain race *mariscolore*: Ireland	96
Chalkhill Blue	*Polyommatus coridon*	Localized resident	100
Adonis Blue	*Polyommatus bellargus*	Localized resident	98
Mazarine Blue	*Cyaniris semiargus*	Former resident (extinct *ca.*1900) [widespread S Europe to Scandinavia]	174
Holly Blue	*Celastrina argiolus*	Common resident race *britanna*: endemic to Britain/Ireland	86
Large Blue	*Glaucopsyche arion*	Extinct 1979 (race *eutyphron*) Re-established resident race *eutyphron*: (from Sweden)	102

English name	Scientific name	Status/notes	Page
Family: LYCAENIDAE – Subfamily: Riodininae			
Duke of Burgundy	*Hamearis lucina*	Localized resident	106
Family: NYMPHALIDAE – Subfamily: Limenitinae			
White Admiral	*Limenitis camilla*	Localized resident	124
Family: NYMPHALIDAE – Subfamily: Apaturinae			
Purple Emperor	*Apatura iris*	Localized resident	126
Family: NYMPHALIDAE – Subfamily: Nymphalinae			
Red Admiral	*Vanessa atalanta*	Annual migrant/breeder from central Europe	128
Painted Lady	*Vanessa cardui*	Annual migrant/breeder from N Africa	130
American Painted Lady	*Vanessa virginiensis*	Vagrant (<100 records; last in 2006) from USA	160
Small Tortoiseshell	*Aglais urticae*	Abundant resident	132
Large Tortoiseshell	*Nymphalis polychloros*	Former resident (extinct *ca.* 1950) Vagrant (approx. 150 records) from continental Europe	184
Scarce Tortoiseshell	*Nymphalis xanthomelas*	Vagrant (one record from 1953 and six or seven seen in 2014) from central and E Europe	182
Camberwell Beauty	*Nymphalis antiopa*	Rare migrant from continental Europe	186
Peacock	*Inachis io*	Abundant resident	134
Comma	*Polygonia c-album*	Common resident	136
Map	*Araschnia levana*	Rare migrant; some records likely released captive-bred butterflies from continental Europe	178
Family: NYMPHALIDAE – Subfamily: Argynninae			
Small Pearl-bordered Fritillary	*Boloria selene*	Declining resident race *selene*: throught Britain except NW Scotland; race *insularum*: NW Scotland	114
Pearl-bordered Fritillary	*Boloria euphrosyne*	Threatened resident	116
Queen of Spain Fritillary	*Issoria lathonia*	Rare migrant/occasional breeder from E and S Europe	180
High Brown Fritillary	*Argynnis adippe*	Threatened resident race *vulgoadippe*: endemic to Britain	118
Dark Green Fritillary	*Argynnis aglaja*	Widespread resident race *aglaja*: England, Wales and S Scotland form *scotica*: N Scotland, Ireland, IoM	120
Silver-washed Fritillary	*Argynnis paphia*	Localized resident	122
Cardinal	*Argynnis pandora*	Vagrant (two records: 1911, 1969) from S Europe	160
Marsh Fritillary	*Euphydryas aurinia*	Threatened resident race *aurinia*: Britain form *hibernica*: Ireland	110

English name	Scientific name	Status/notes	Page
Glanville Fritillary	*Melitaea cinxia*	Rare resident	*112*
Heath Fritillary	*Melitaea athalia*	Threatened resident	*108*
Family: NYMPHALIDAE – Subfamily: Satyrinae			
Speckled Wood	*Pararge aegeria*	Common resident race *tircis*: Britain and Ireland race *oblita*: Scotland race *insula*: Isles of Scilly	*140*
Wall	*Lasiommata megera*	Localized resident	*142*
Mountain Ringlet	*Erebia epiphron*	Localized resident race *mnemon*: England race *scotica*: Scotland	*152*
Scotch Argus	*Erebia aethiops*	Localized resident race *aethiops*: England and N Scotland race *caledonia*: S and W Scotland	*154*
Arran Brown	*Erebia ligea*	Status unknown/Possible resident specimens attributed to NW Scotland found in collections as recently as 1969	*190*
Marbled White	*Melanargia galathea*	Widespread resident race *serena*: endemic to British Isles	*138*
Grayling	*Hipparchia semele*	Declining resident race *semele*: England and Wales race *thyone*: Great Orme, Conwy race *scota*: W, SW & E Scotland and NE England race *atlantica*: NW Scotland race *hibernica*: Ireland except The Burren race *clarensis*: The Burren, Ireland	*144*
Gatekeeper	*Pyronia tithonus*	Common resident race *britanniae*: endemic to Britain and Ireland	*146*
Meadow Brown	*Maniola jurtina*	Abundant resident race *insularis*: throughout Britain except race *splendida*: NW Scotland + Isle of Man race *iernes*: Ireland race *cassiteridium*: Isles of Scilly	*148*
Small Heath	*Coenonympha pamphilus*	Abundant resident race *pamphilus*: Britain and Ireland race *rhoumensis*: Isle of Rhum	*156*
Large Heath	*Coenonympha tullia*	Declining resident race *davus*: NW England and N Wales race *polydama*: N England, W Wales and Ireland race *scotica*: N Scotland	*158*
Ringlet	*Aphantopus hyperantus*	Widespread resident	*150*
Family: NYMPHALIDAE – Subfamily: Danainae			
Monarch	*Danaus plexippus*	Rare migrant from USA and possibly from established population in S Europe and the Macaronesian islands	*188*

Butterfly watching and photography

The Victorian hobby of butterfly collecting has been largely replaced by butterfly photography. Recently at Fermyn Woods, on a hot day in early July, there must have been over 40 visiting photographers. Their objective was not to capture the Purple Emperor itself, as our predecessors would have tried to do, but to capture digital images of this magnificent butterfly. Because these woods cover a wide area, this number of enthusiasts could easily be accommodated.

When looking for a rare species, it helps to have other people present because word soon passes between groups about the best places to be looking and how to achieve the best images. There is an unwritten code of conduct that you do not step in front of someone else's view or disturb a settled insect if you can possibly avoid doing so. Everyone then enjoys themselves and (usually) takes away images that will continue that enjoyment for many years to come.

To be successful when there are not so many people about, it is extremely helpful to know where to begin looking. The more you know about a butterfly's ecology, its choice of nectar plants, its caterpillar's foodplants, where it lays its eggs, how the two sexes relate to each other and their different behaviours, the easier it will be to find a rare species in the wild. Hopefully this book will provide the information you need. Then, if you want to seek out a particular butterfly, as many people enjoy doing, you must follow your clues (and, of course, the weather).

Robin Page once wrote a colourful book (see *page 235*) on his adventures finding every one of our resident and regular migrant species in a single season. It was a massive task and, like most challenges, others have done the same thing. But most people will not have the time or inclination to follow this path, and instead will be content with simply enjoying butterflies in their gardens or nearby countryside. As the section opposite describes, recording butterflies wherever you are is important because national records are made up from thousands of individual returns sent in by dedicated people who enjoy what they see and are willing to spend a little time keeping records.

Good compact cameras with zoom lenses are readily available and can produce remarkably good results. However, serious close-up photography really requires a DSLR (digital single-lens reflex) camera, which allows you to use different close-up or macro lenses and obtain really high-quality results. There are now many good books on insect photography but Robert Thompson's book, first published in 2005 (see *page 234*), set a new standard for the reproduction of high-quality images.

For those who do not want to wrestle with cameras, and even for those who do, a pair of close-focus binoculars will be invaluable. Many of our butterflies are quite small and the extra magnification that binoculars give allows you to get a much closer view without having to get too close and possibly disturbing your prize.

Butterfly Conservation

Founded in 1968, **Butterfly Conservation** is the UK charity dedicated to saving butterflies and moths and their habitats. It runs a wide variety of conservation projects, and is taking the lead in protecting the UK's butterfly and moth populations, particularly through research on population trends and by the preparation of detailed Action Plans to reverse population declines. These plans are implemented in close collaboration with statutory and voluntary conservation organisations, as well as with corporate partners and individuals. Much of this work is conducted at a landscape scale to ensure long-term conservation of threatened species, with over 70 landscapes prioritised for action.

In addition, Butterfly Conservation manages over 30 nature reserves and gives advice on over 50 partnership reserves owned by others. A strong membership supports regional branches throughout the UK. Every year, these branches organize hundreds of field trips, talks, and educational courses. Volunteers are involved in monitoring several thousand important localities, and give practical help by attending work-parties to manage habitats.

Members are kept up-to-date by the charity's magazine *Butterfly* and a steady stream of reports and papers is available covering detailed scientific news and research. Local branches also produce their own regular newsletters and run their own websites which list events and projects in their area. A wealth of information and links to the Branch websites are available from Butterfly Conservation's website **www.butterfly-conservation.org**.

Recording and monitoring

A central aspect of Butterfly Conservation's work is the gathering of accurate recording and monitoring information on the state of butterflies and moths. The *Butterflies for the New Millennium* recording scheme is the largest of its kind in the world, with over seven million records gathered from over 10,000 recorders across Britain and Ireland. The results have been used to produce *The Millennium Atlas of Butterflies in Britain and Ireland*, and subsequent updates on the *State of Britain's Butterflies*. In 2007, Butterfly Conservation also launched the *National Moth Recording Scheme* that has already gathered over 18 million records of larger moths.

The UK Butterfly Monitoring Scheme gathers data on population trends from a network of over 1,200 sites across the UK, chiefly based on weekly counts from butterfly transects. The dataset comprises over 16 million records gathered since 1973. The results have been used to create Governmental Butterfly Indicators that help measure the state of the environment and biodiversity. Thanks to the scheme, a huge amount has also been discovered about the ecology of butterflies and how habitat management and the weather affect their populations.

Information on these schemes and how to take part are available on the Butterfly Conservation website as well as **www.ukbms.org.uk** and **www.mothscount.org**.

Conservation and legislation

The Red List

Data obtained from both UKBMS and BNM have been used to draw up the *Butterfly Red List for Great Britain*. This classifies species according to their relative risk of extinction based upon rarity, trend in their population size (whether they are getting more or less rare) and the threats that they face.

The Red List categories were devised by the International Union for Conservation of Nature (IUCN) and have been accepted internationally. The categories are REGIONALLY EXTINCT (in our case, the region is Britain), CRITICALLY ENDANGERED, ENDANGERED, VULNERABLE, NEAR THREATENED, and Least Concern.

It is a sobering fact that 19 of the 59 butterfly species that breed in Britain and Ireland today are included in one of the 'threat' categories (*i.e.* CRITICALLY ENDANGERED, ENDANGERED or VULNERABLE) and a further 11 are categorized as NEAR THREATENED. That equates to over 50% of our breeding species. In addition, four species have become extinct as breeding species in historical times. The species listed in each of the categories are as follows (in all cases the species are listed in alphabetical order):

REGIONALLY EXTINCT: Black-veined White, Large Copper, Large Tortoiseshell, Mazarine Blue.

CRITICALLY ENDANGERED: Large Blue, High Brown Fritillary.

ENDANGERED: Black Hairstreak, Chequered Skipper, Duke of Burgundy, Glanville Fritillary, Heath Fritillary, Pearl-bordered Fritillary, White-letter Hairstreak, Wood White.

VULNERABLE: Brown Hairstreak, Dingy Skipper, Grayling, Grizzled Skipper, Large Heath, Marsh Fritillary, Northern Brown Argus, Silver-studded Blue, White Admiral.

NEAR THREATENED: Adonis Blue, Chalkhill Blue, Lulworth Skipper, Mountain Ringlet, Purple Emperor, Silver-spotted Skipper, Small Blue, Small Heath, Small Pearl-bordered Fritillary, Swallowtail, Wall.

UK Biodiversity Action Plan

Under the UK's Biodiversity Action Plan (UKBAP) **www.ukbap.org.uk**, a list of priorities has been drawn up which recognizes the practical issues of conservation and establishes priorities. This is the Government's response to world concern about nature conservation and our international obligations under the United Nations. A *Priority Species* identified in the UKBAP is one that is both globally threatened and declining rapidly in the UK. When deciding what to do about such a threatened species, many factors have to be considered, like the chances of achieving a recovery, its cost and benefits to other species, and our national and international obligations.

The UKBAP identifies 24 butterfly species as Priority Species. These are:
Brown Hairstreak, Chequered Skipper, Dingy Skipper, Duke of Burgundy, Glanville Fritillary, Grayling, Grizzled Skipper, Heath Fritillary, High Brown Fritillary, Large Blue, Large Heath, Lulworth Skipper, Marsh Fritillary, Mountain Ringlet, Northern Brown Argus, Pearl-bordered Fritillary, Silver-studded Blue, Small Blue, Small Heath, Small Pearl-bordered Fritillary, White Admiral, White-letter Hairstreak, Wall and Wood White. They are all on the Red List

in one or other category. Butterfly Conservation is Lead Partner for all these species, taking action to conserve them and co-ordinating the efforts of others.

Finally, Local Biodiversity Action Plans have been produced by many local authorities and other bodies. These aim to deliver conservation action at a local level. Butterflies are targeted in many of these plans, which provide opportunities for anyone to take part in surveys, monitoring or more practical conservation action.

European and domestic legislation

As with many other wildlife groups, the butterfly fauna of the British Isles is an impoverished version of that found in continental Europe. Nevertheless, the populations of some species have declined significantly and/or are highly localized at the European scale. For these species, EU and domestic legislation offers some protection, especially through requirements to conserve their habitats. The relevant legal protection is summarized in the red 'Status and protection' boxes in the main species accounts (see *page 41* for explanation) and further details are given below.

Three species – Marsh Fritillary, Large Blue and Large Copper (which sadly is now extinct in Britain) – are listed in Annex II and/or Annex IV of the EU Habitats Directive and in Appendix II of the Council for Europe Bern Convention on the Conservation of European Wildlife and Natural Habitats. This requires governments to take action to protect these species and their habitats.

In the UK, six species – Heath Fritillary, High Brown Fritillary, Large Blue, Large Copper, Marsh Fritillary and Swallowtail – are listed in Schedule 5 of the Wildlife and Countryside Act 1981 (shown as 'W&C Act: FULL PROTECTION' in the red box in the species accounts) and are thus conferred some degree of protection by prohibiting handling without a licence. A further 19 species – Adonis Blue, Black Hairstreak, Brown Hairstreak, Chalkhill Blue, Chequered Skipper, Duke of Burgundy, Glanville Fritillary, Large Heath, Large Tortoiseshell, Lulworth Skipper, Mountain Ringlet, Northern Brown Argus, Pearl-bordered Fritillary, Purple Emperor, Silver-spotted Skipper, Silver-studded Blue, Small Blue, White-letter Hairstreak and Wood White – are covered by Section 9, Part 5 of the W&C Act 1981, which prohibits their sale without a licence (these are shown as 'W&C Act: SALE PROHIBITED' in the red box in the species accounts).

Section 14(1) of the Wildlife and Countryside Act 1981 makes it illegal to release or allow to escape into the wild any animal that is not ordinarily resident in Great Britain and is not a regular visitor to Great Britain in a wild state. Thus, deliberate releases of non-native butterflies into the countryside is an offence that could lead to prosecution.

Also under the Wildlife and Countrtyside Act 1981, a suite of Sites of Special Scientific Interest (SSSI) has been notified, including key sites selected for their rare breeding species or outstanding assemblages of species.

In Ireland, seven species – Brimstone, Dingy Skipper, Holly Blue, Large Heath, Marsh Fritillary, Purple Hairstreak and Small Blue – are listed on Schedules 5 & 7 and afforded full protection under Sections 10 and 13 of the Wildlife (Northern Ireland) Order 1985.

Further reading

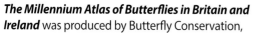

Discover Butterflies in Britain is a companion book for this one, published by **WILD**Guides and also written by David Newland. It focusses on where to find butterflies in Britain and has detailed site descriptions supported by maps and photographs of key places to see all our breeding species. There is specific guidance about when and where to look for each butterfly and the directions should guide you to every rare species if you decide to search for them.

The Millennium Atlas of Butterflies in Britain and Ireland was produced by Butterfly Conservation, in conjunction with the Biological Records Office of the Centre for Ecology and Hydrology, and the Dublin Naturalists' Field Club, and is published by Oxford University Press. It is not only a beautiful book to browse through, but also an outstanding and authoritative work of reference. The text is by Jim Asher, Martin Warren, Richard Fox, Paul Harding, Gail Jeffcoate and Stephen Jeffcoate.

The State of Butterflies in Britain and Ireland is an update produced in 2006 by the same three organisations. This is published by Pisces Publications for Butterfly Conservation. The authors are Richard Fox, Jim Asher, Tom Brereton, David Roy and Martin Warren.

The most readable book on Britain's butterflies to have been produced in the last fifty years is **The Butterflies of Britain & Ireland** by Jeremy Thomas and Richard Lewington. Nobody knows Britain's butterflies better than Professor Thomas, and his essays on each species are a delight. The illustrations are by Richard Lewington, Britain's leading butterfly artist. A new edition was published in 2014 by British Wildlife Publishing.

As a scientific work of reference, **The Butterflies of Great Britain and Ireland**, edited by A. Maitland Emmet and John Heath, published by Harley Books in 1990, is unchallenged. This is one volume of a series on moths and butterflies and covers all the butterflies ever recorded in Britain. The superb plates are, once again, by Richard Lewington. Unfortunately it is now becoming dated because it does not include the most recent information.

An authoritative treatment of Northern Ireland's butterfly fauna is given in **The Butterflies and Moths of Northern Ireland** by Robert Thompson and Brian Nelson, published by National Museums Northern Ireland in 2006. Although this is a large and expensive book, it has extremely high quality images. Robert Thompson has also written **Close-up and Macro - a Photographer's Guide**, published by David & Charles in 2005, which provides an excellent introduction to taking close-up pictures and explains why the standard in his other book is so high.

British and Irish Butterflies by Adrian Riley, published by Brambleby Books in 2007, describes all the recognised British subspecies, and shows how butterflies of the same species may look different in different parts of the country and where they may be found. This gives us over 100 subspecies to track down in Britain and Ireland.

If that is not enough, there are several good guides to European butterflies. Tristan Lafranchis' *Butterflies of Europe* is an excellent field guide (in English). It was published in 2004 in France by Diatheo. Lafranchis is also the principal author and editor of *Les Papillons de jour de France, Belgique et Luxembourg et leurs chenilles*, published by Biotope. This has excellent photographs and clear text (written in French). There is also *Collins Field Guide: Butterflies of Britain & Europe,* with text by Tom Tolman and more splendid illustrations by Richard Lewington.

The Royal Entomological Society's Handbook, vol 12, part 6, *Checklist of the Lepidoptera of the British Isles* by David J.L. Agassiz, Stella D. Beavan and Robert J. Heckford was published in 2013. This is the 'official' list of all our butterfly species, subspecies and forms in taxonomic order. It includes species that cannot be regarded as definitely part of our fauna, and are probably unlikely to recur, such as those imported or released by accident.

Lastly, for an enjoyable read, try Robin Page's *The Great British Butterfly Safari*, Bird's Farm Books, 2003 and Patrick Barkham's *The Butterfly Isles*, Granta Books, 2011. Both tell of their author's quests to see all our different species for themselves. Patrick Barkham's book has an accompanying DVD *Guide to British Butterflies*.

Sources of further information and useful addresses

Butterfly Conservation
Manor Yard, East Lulworth, Wareham, Dorset BH20 5QP.
info@butterfly-conservation.org
www.butterfly-conservation.org

Butterfly Monitoring Scheme
Managed by Butterfly Conservation
www.ukbms.org

The Wildlife Trusts
The Kiln Waterside, Mather Road, Newark, Nottinghamshire NG24 1WT.
enquiry@wildlifetrusts.org
www.wildlifetrusts.org

The Dublin Naturalists' Field Club
Honorary Secretary, Gerry Sharkey, 81 Jamestown Road, Finglas, Dublin 11.
dnfc@eircom.net
www.dnfc.net

UK Plant Health Service
The Food and Environment Research Agency, Sand Hutton, York YO41 1LZ.
planthealth.info@fera.gsi.gov.uk
www.fera.defra.gov.uk

De Vlinderstichting – Dutch Butterfly Conservation
Postbus 506, 6700 AM Wageningen, The Netherlands.
www.vlinderstichting.nl

UK Butterflies
www.ukbutterflies.co.uk
A comprehensive site dealing with all UK butterfly species, taxonomic issues, sightings, events and resources, which is updated regularly with the latest news and photographs.

European Butterflies
www.pyrgus.de
Contains excellent images of the majority of European butterflies, including their immature stages, and hints on ecology and life history.

Acknowledgements and photographic/artwork credits

As for the two previous editions, the production of this book has been a group activity and is the combined effort of David Newland, Robert Still and Andy Swash, with the generous help of many people, to whom we are very grateful. We continue to receive great support from Butterfly Conservation and thank its Chief Executive, Martin Warren, for endorsing the book with his Foreword. We have also benefitted from the generous cooperation of Dutch Butterfly Conservation in providing information about European species. We would like to thank Gill Swash and Brian Clews for their contribution in editing and proof-reading the book respectively, and Peter Eeles and Rob Hume for providing helpful comments.

We have of course drawn from the vast literature, particularly that listed under *Further reading* (*page 234*), and have been helped greatly by the information gleaned from many websites, and particularly from **www.ukbutterflies.co.uk** and **www.pyrgus.de**. Site information is given as fully as space allows; further details of many sites are given in **WILD**Guides" companion book *Discover Butterflies in Britain*, **www.discoverbutterflies.com**. We are very grateful to all those who helped by allowing us to use their photographs for this new edition, particularly Peter Eeles, Wolfgang Wagner, Rob de Jost, Chris van Swaay and those who provided additional photographs under the generous terms of the *Creative Commons licences*, details of which are available from **https://creativecommons. org/licenses/by-sa/2.0/**, and the Wikimedia Commons *Creative Commons Attribution-Share Alike 3.0 Unported license*, details of which are available from **http://creativecommons.org/ licenses/by-sa/3.0/legalcode**. We have endeavoured to ensure that the list that follows is complete, but if we discover errors or omissions we can only apologise and undertake to correct these as soon as practicable.

We hope that readers will find this book helpful and enjoyable. Your interest will help to conserve these fragile insects for future generations. Please consider joining the very worthwhile charity Butterfly Conservation (see *page 231*), which is dedicated to that objective.

The production of this book would not have been possible without the help and co-operation of the photographers whose images have been reproduced. The plates are one of the key features of the book and we would like to acknowledge the skill and patience of the photographers listed below who kindly allowed us to use their work. Although the majority of the photographs in this book were taken by one of us [DN], all the other photographs are specifically credited on the following pages. Some 56 photographers have contributed their images to the book and they are listed here in alphabetical order by surname (the initials in square brackets are those used in the individual photo credits).

Alan Barnes [AB]; Les Borg (Windrush Photos) [LB]; Colin Carver (Windrush Photos) [CC]; Alan Cassidy [AC]; Drahkrub (Wikimedia Commons) [D/WC]; Dendroica cerulea (Creative Commons) [D/CC]; Stefano Douneika (Creative Commons) [SD/CC]; Sean Edwards [SE]; Peter Eeles (**ukbutterflies. co.uk**) [PE]; Thomas Ennis (Windrush Photos) [TE]; Simon Eugster (Wikimedia Commons) [SE/WC]; Gianpiero Ferrari [GF]; Petr Filippov (Wikimedia Commons) [PF/WC]; Christian Fischer (Wikimedia Commons) [CF/WC]; Alec Harmer (Natural Image) [AH]; Barry Hilling [BH]; Tony Hoare [TH]; John Holloway [JH]; Rob de Jost (**farmlator.hu**) [RdJ]; Paul Kipling [PK]; Fredrik Lähnn (Wikimedia Commons) [FL/WC]; Matt Lavin (Creative Commons) [ML/CC]; James K. Lindsey (Wikimedia Commons) [JL/WC]; Gilles San Martin (Wikimedia Commons) [GM/CC]; Vince Massimo [VM];

George McCarthy (Windrush Photos) [GM]; David Newland [DN]; Dennis Paulson [DP]; Kristian Peters (Wikimedia Commons) [KP/WC]; Alan Petty (Windrush Photos) [AP]; Petr Filippov (Wikimedia Commons) [PF/WC]; Rasbak (Wikimedia Commons) [R/WC]; Richard Revels (Windrush Photos) [RR]; Harry Rose (Creative Commons) [HR/CC]; Anneli Salo (Wikimedia Commons) [AS/WC]; Sannse (Wikimedia Commons) [S/WC]; Rudolf Schäfer (Creative Commons) [RS/CC]; Joan Simon (Creative Commons) [JS/CC]; Dave Smallshire [DS]; Anya Still [AS]; Robert Still [RS]; Malcolm Storey (**bioimages.org.uk**) [MS]; Chris van Swaay / Dutch Butterfly Conservation (**vlinderstichting.nl**) [CvS]; Andy & Gill Swash (**WorldWildlifeImages.com**) [A&GS]; Jeremy Thomas [JT]; Tigerente (Wikimedia Commons) [T/WC]; Tubifex (Wikimedia Commons) [T/WC]; David Tipling [DT]; Graham Titchmarsh [GT]; Wolfgang Wagner (**pyrgus.de**) [WW]; Martin Warren [MW]; Ken Willmott [KW]; Wikimedia Commons [WC]; Willow (Wikimedia Commons) [W/WC]; Peter J Wilson [PJW] and H. Zell (Wikimedia Commons) [HZ/WC]; Zirpe (Wikimedia Commons) [Z/WC].

SPECIES OF DOUBTFUL PROVENANCE

Page 192: Sooty Copper: A&GS.
Moorland Clouded Yellow: GM/CC (flickr.com/photos/sanmartin/3788620326/).
Page 193: Oberthür's Grizzled Skipper: A&GS. Green-underside Blue: DS. Western Dappled White: DS. Large Wall: A&GS. False Grayling A&GS.

CATERPILLAR FOODPLANTS

Page 194: Common Nettle: RS. Hop: HZ/WC (commons.wikimedia.org/wiki/File:Humulus_lupulus_007.JPG).
Page 195: Narrow-leaved Everlasting-pea: AS/WC (commons.wikimedia.org/wiki/File:Lathyrus_sylvestris_Metsänätkelmä_H5384_C.jpg). Kidney Vetch, Meadow Vetchling: RS. Lucerne: ML/CC (flickr.com/photos/plant_diversity/5182318891). Horseshoe Vetch: T/WC (commons.wikimedia.org/wiki/File:Hippocrepis_comosa.jpg). Tufted Vetch: RS. Red Clover: SE. Common Bird's-foot-trefoil: FL/WC (commons.wikimedia.org/wiki/File:Lotus_corniculatus11.JPG).
Page 196: Field Pansy, Common Dog-violet, Charlock, Wild Mignonette, Water-cress: RS. Hedge Mustard: HZ/WC (commons.wikimedia.org/wiki/File:Sisymbrium_officinale_001.JPG). Garlic Mustard, Cuckooflower: A&GS. Nasturtium: Tu/WC (http://commons.wikimedia.org/wiki/File:3853_-_Tropaeolum_majus_(Große_Kapuzinerkresse).JPG).
Page 197: Honeysuckle: A&GS. Willow: W/WC (commons.wikimedia.org/wiki/File:Salix_alba_002.jpg). Blackthorn: AS. Oak: SE/WC (commons.wikimedia.org/wiki/File:Quercus_robur_early_flowers.jpg). Holly & Ivy: RS. Alder Buckthorn: A&GS. Elm: WC (http://commons.wikimedia.org/wiki/File:English_elm_leaves.jpg). Bilberry, Gorse: A&GS. Broom: RS/CC (flickr.com/photos/schaefer-rudolf/8687720905).
Page 198: Milk-parsley: F/WC (commons.wikimedia.org/wiki/File:Peucedanum_palustre2.jpg). Crane's-bill, Thyme, Silverweed, Strawberry, Agrimony: RS.
Page 199: Thistle, scabious, Foxglove, Primrose, Cowslip: A&GS. Plantain: S/WC (commons.wikimedia.org/wiki/File:Ribwort_600.jpg). Cow-wheat: JS/CC (flickr.com/photos/simonjoan/2483710913). Speedwell, Sorrel, Rock-rose: RS.
Page 200: Soft-grass: R/WC (commons.wikimedia.org/wiki/File:Gladde_witbol_bloeiwijze_Holcus_mollis.jpg#file). Yorkshire-fog: HR/CC (flickr.com/photos/macleaygrassman/7325959434). Couch: D/CC (flickr.com/photos/dendroica/8964381180). Timothy, bottom scene: RS. Cock's-foot: A&GS. Tor Grass: D/WC (commons.wikimedia.org/wiki/File:Brachypodium_pinnatum-(dkrb)-1.jpg). Hair-grass: CF/WC (commons.wikimedia.org/wiki/File:DeschampsiaCespitosa1.jpg). False Brome: KP/WC (commons.wikimedia.org/wiki/File:Brachypodium_sylvaticum.jpeg).
Page 201: Red Fescue: HL/WC (http://commons.wikimedia.org/wiki/File:Festuca.rubra.2.jpg). Sheep's-fescue: R/WC (commons.wikimedia.org/wiki/File:Ruig_schapengras_bloeiwijze_(Festuca_ovina_subsp._hirtula).jpg). Downy Oat-grass: PF/WC (http://commons.wikimedia.org/wiki/File:Avenula_pubescens1.JPG). Common Bent: R/WC (http://commons.wikimedia.org/wiki/File:Gewoon_struisgras_bloeiwijze_Agrostis_tenuis.jpg). Purple Moor-grass: Z/WC (http://commons.wikimedia.org/wiki/File:Molinia.jpg). Blue Moor-grass: PF/WC (http://commons.wikimedia.org/wiki/File:Sesleria_caerulea1.JPG). Bristle Bent: MS. Meadow-grass: RS.

EGGS, CATERPILLARS AND CHRYSALISES

All early life stage photos on **pages 206–224** *are by RR except the following:*

Eggs
Page 207: **Black-veined White:** PE. **Bath White:** WW. **Berger's** & **Pale Clouded Yellows:** WW.
Page 208: **Monarch:** PE. **Large Blue:** MW. **Mazarine Blue:** PE. **Long-tailed Blue:** PE. **Short-tailed Blue:** WW.
Page 209: **Glanville Fritillary:** TH. **Dark Green Fritillary:** MW.
Page 210: **Green Hairstreak:** AH. **Red Admiral, PE.** **Map:** PE.
Page 211: **Speckled Wood:** AH. **Grayling, Meadow Brown** & **Ringlet:** KW. **Arran Brown:** WW.

Caterpillars
Page 212: **Brimstone:** MW. **Small White:** PE. **Cryptic Wood White** (artwork): RS.
Page 213: **Large White:** LB. **Swallowtail** (young): PE. **Monarch:** PE.
Page 214: **Small Skipper:** KW. **Brown Hairstreak:** PE.
Page 215: **Large Blue:** JT. **Mazarine Blue:** WW. **Short-tailed Blue:** PE. **Long-tailed Blue:** PE.
Page 216: **Queen of Spain Fritillary:** GF. **Map:** PE.
Page 217: **Comma:** A&GS. **Large Tortoiseshell:** AB. **Camberwell Beauty:** PE. **Scarce Tortoiseshell:** PE.
Page 218: **Gatekeeper:** GF. **Arran Brown:** WW.

Chrysalises
Page 219: **Brimstone:** GM. **Berger's Clouded Yellow** (artwork): RS. **Large White:** PE. **Small White:** TH. **Orange-tip:** GF. **Cryptic Wood White** (artwork): RS. **Bath White:** PE.
Page 220: **Small Skipper:** KW. **Green Hairstreak, Brown Hairstreak, Purple Hairstreak:** GF.
Page 221: **Small Blue, Northern Brown Argus:** AH. **Silver-studded Blue, Adonis Blue:** KW. **Large Blue:** MW. **Short-tailed Blue:** PE. **Long-tailed Blue:** PE. **Mazarine Blue:** WW.
Page 221: **Queen of Spain Fritillary:** GF.
Page 222: **Map:** PE.
Page 223: **Comma, Peacock, Large Tortoiseshell:** GF. **Camberwell Beauty:** PE.
Page 224: **Marbled White:** PE. **Wall:** GF. **Arran Brown:** WW. **Monarch:** PE.

Index of English and scientific names

This index includes the common English and scientific names of all the butterflies mentioned in this book.
The **names in bold** highlight the species currently known to breed in Britain or Ireland.
Bold figures refer to the main species account.
Italicized figures relate to the page(s) on which a photograph may be found, colour-coding being used to indicate whether the photograph is of an egg, caterpillar, chrysalis or an adult.
Normal black figures relate to other page(s) on which key information is given.